THE EPISCOPAL COLLEAGUES OF
ARCHBISHOP THOMAS BECKET

THE
EPISCOPAL COLLEAGUES OF
ARCHBISHOP THOMAS BECKET

BEING THE FORD LECTURES
DELIVERED IN THE UNIVERSITY OF OXFORD
IN HILARY TERM 1949

BY

DAVID KNOWLES, F.B.A.

*Professor of Medieval History in the
University of Cambridge*

CAMBRIDGE
AT THE UNIVERSITY PRESS
1951

PUBLISHED BY
THE SYNDICS OF THE CAMBRIDGE UNIVERSITY PRESS

London Office: Bentley House, N.W.1
American Branch: New York

Agents for Canada, India and Pakistan: Macmillan

Printed in Great Britain at The Carlyle Press, Birmingham 6

CONTENTS

APPENDICES

PREFACE

THE chapters of this book reproduce with a few slight changes the text prepared for delivery as the Ford Lectures in the first months of 1949. Actually, a very slow delivery was found unavoidable, and in consequence matter equal to at least one-sixth of the whole was omitted, chiefly from the account of the doings of the bishops during the exile of Archbishop Thomas.

An invitation to deliver the Ford Lectures has often been made the occasion for presenting the result of many years of laborious scholarship in a specialized field, and the resulting publication has been a book of great and permanent value. Other lecturers, for this reason or that, have had in mind more directly the audience of the day. The present writer found himself obliged, for various reasons, to adopt the second of these two courses, and the lectures are now published mainly out of deference to a convention, and without modification of style or treatment. This applies particularly to the final chapter, which aims at giving no more than a single aspect of the great controversy. A full treatment would have to take account of all the political and social issues which were present at the time, less explicitly perhaps but none the less powerfully, in the minds of men. As, however, the topic with which the lectures deal abounds in critical problems, great and small, of dates and persons and sources, it seemed useless to print the text without an apparatus of footnotes. In such a field as this any acquisition of knowledge, however small, may help a student who comes after.

I hope that I have acknowledged in the notes the assistance given me by friends at Oxford and elsewhere. The text and notes, when prepared for press, were read and criticized, with infinite care, by Mr. C. N. L. Brooke, to my very great profit. If I do not acknowledge specifically every change dictated by his learning and scholarship it is only because the iteration of such acknowledgment would be as tedious to him as to my readers. I cannot, however, refrain from mentioning that his criticisms both provoked and emended Appendices III, IV and V.

An interval of several months between the delivery and annotation of the lectures has allowed a certain space for reflection on the attitude and conduct of the bishops. I think it is true to say that, after such reflection, their acceptance without demur of Gregorian principles of church government, and in particular of the paramount duty of obedience to their metropolitan and to the Pope, appears to me very striking. The judgments of Tout, in his otherwise valuable and suggestive essay, that 'most of the bishops were on the king's side' and, still more emphatically, that there was 'solid support given by the English bishops to the king', are surely not tenable.[1] Had Archbishop Thomas not failed them at Clarendon and—perhaps a still more weighty circumstance—had Gilbert Foliot not lent his name and ability to a defence of the king's case (it would not be true to say, of the king's cause) there is no reason to suppose that the solidarity of the bishops would have been broken down in 1163-4. And I am now inclined to attribute this solidarity somewhat less exclusively than in the last pages of these lectures to the influence of Archbishop Theobald, and more confidently to the acceptance by the bishops of post-Gregorian papal government, in theory and in practice, as they had learnt it in the schools, and experienced it in their lives.

PETERHOUSE   DAVID KNOWLES
24 November 1949

[1] T. F. Tout, 'The Place of St Thomas of Canterbury in History', in *Bulletin of the John Rylands Library*, VI (1921), 253, 244.

CHAPTER I

THE BISHOPS OF THE CONTROVERSY (1)

(i)

THE celebrated conflict between Henry II and Archbishop Thomas of Canterbury has received comparatively little attention from English historians during the past fifty years. In part this has been due to a natural inclination to let a heavily cropped soil lie fallow. During the second half of the nineteenth century the reign of Henry II was intensively studied by numerous scholars, of whom Stubbs and Maitland were the most eminent, and the outline of the ecclesiastical controversy was retailed by E. A. Freeman, R. H. Froude, J. R. Green, Kate Norgate, Sir J. H. Ramsay and a score of lesser writers and controversialists. Though it cannot be said that a final equilibrium of opinion was reached, a kind of *via media* was struck out, which has since been repeated in numberless manuals. A feeling developed that the topic had been exhausted, and even that it was a sterile one.

Among professional historians, moreover, reasons of a more technical kind have had their weight. The literary and official sources of information on the controversy are voluminous, and so far as is known they now exist for the most part in print; the form, however, in which they are available is very far from satisfactory. The great corpus of lives and letters published towards the end of the last century, and filling nine bulky volumes of the Rolls Series, is very difficult material to use.[1] As regards the biographical collection,

---

[1] *Materials for the History of Archbishop Thomas Becket* (Rolls Series, 67), 7 vols, 1875-85. These are made up as follows: 1. Life and Miracles by William of Canterbury; 2. Lives by Benedict of

the editors made no serious attempt to establish the relationship between the lives, or to date them accurately; yet without such critical foundations the unwary historian may continually find himself treating as separate pieces of evidence what are in fact copies of a single witness, or quoting as an eye-witness's testimony what in fact is derived from an earlier account. With the letters the case is even worse. Few of them bear any mark of dating, and many of them lack also any internal indication of time; only by slow and very careful criticism could an editor, long familiar with the events and steeped in the literary monuments and at home with all the personalities and currents of opinion, hope to establish a reliable chronological sequence; yet without this the collection may easily become a jungle full of pitfalls and sloughs, all the more so since no adequate index has been compiled for either letters or lives. The editors of the volumes of *Materials* in the Rolls Series—Canon Robertson, and, for the last volume, Dr J. B. Sheppard—were industrious and conscientious, but they lacked the vast learning of Stubbs and the specialized knowledge of R. L. Poole, and they were debarred by the narrow instructions governing the Rolls editors from furnishing critical discussions of dates and persons. Consequently, it has to be said that the reader can ill afford to neglect the scrutiny of any document that does not bear an explicit date. It should in fairness be added that Canon Robertson had set himself

Peterborough, John of Salisbury, Alan of Tewkesbury and Edward Grim; 3. Lives by William Fitz-Stephen and Herbert of Bosham; 4. Lives by Anonymous I and Anonymous II, the Quadrilogus, and other relevant documents; 5-7. Letters. The editor, Canon J. C. Robertson, died before the last volume was printed; it was completed by Dr J. B. Sheppard. To these volumes must be added the Icelandic *Thomas Saga Erkibyskups*, edited by Eiríkr Magnússon (Rolls Series, 65), 2 vols, 1875-83.

an impossible task. Very **many** important items in the great dossier come from the letter-books of Gilbert Foliot[1] and John of Salisbury,[2] and both of these, as printed by Giles in the mid-nineteenth century and never since re-edited, are a chaos. Before any attempt could be made at a wholesale rearrangement of the Becket materials, critical editions of Foliot and John of Salisbury are an absolute necessity. It is pleasant to know that both of these enterprises are in train.[3]

In the opening words of this lecture my remarks were of set purpose restricted to English historians. The most valuable critical work on the sources in recent years has in fact been done in France by M. Walberg, a disciple of M. Halphen, whose own essay on the subject had appeared some years earlier.[4] M. Walberg has provided future editors of the Lives with critical prolegomena, and his edition of the important French metrical life by Guernes de Pont Sainte Maxence, omitted from the Rolls Series, is a model of its kind.[5] Finally, Mlle Raymonde Foreville, using this and

[1] *Gilberti Foliot Epistolae*, ed. J. A. Giles, 2 vols, Oxford, 1846.

[2] *Joannis Saresberiensis Opera Omnia*, vol i, *Epistolae*, ed. J. A. Giles, Oxford, 1848.

[3] An edition of Foliot's letters was planned by the late Professor Z. N. Brooke, in collaboration with Dom Adrian Morey. The work is being continued by Dom Morey and Mr C. N. L. Brooke. The text of the letters of John of Salisbury has been prepared by an American scholar, Fr Miller, S.J., and is to appear in the series of *Medieval Classics* edited by Professors V. H. Galbraith and R. A. B. Mynors.

[4]'Les Biographes de Thomas Becket' in *Revue Historique*, LII (1909), 35-45. This, however, has been wholly superseded by later work.

[5] *La Vie de S. Thomas le Martyr par Guernes de Pont-Sainte-Maxence*, ed. E. Walberg, Lund, 1922. The introduction summarizes the findings of the editor published previously in various studies, to which references are given, but these articles and several later ones are reprinted by M. Walberg in *La tradition hagiographique de saint Thomas Becket avant la fin du xiie siècle*, Paris, 1929

other recent material, has presented the controversy in ample form in a work which cannot be neglected even by those who do not feel it to be absolutely definitive.[1]

Having said so much as to the state of the sources, I may be thought to have shown the futility of approaching the subject at all. A study on the grand scale would indeed, until the editors have done their work, require many years of patient labour. The controversy was, however, one which drew into its orbit many distinguished men of the time; though in the past it has almost invariably been considered as a straightforward narrative of the life of a single man, it has in fact many facets, and the illumination of a number of these might provide new and more subtle colours for the use of a biographer of the archbishop. It is with one of these facets that these lectures will be concerned.

(ii)

The episcopal colleagues of Archbishop Thomas were a remarkable group of men, and it is surprising that they have received so little attention collectively, and that only two of their number should have been the objects of study as individuals. Of these prelates, all save three have found a place in the *Dictionary of National Biography*, and for the omission of one of these three—Jocelin of Salisbury—no ready explanation suggests itself, unless it be the difficulty of establishing his genealogy and early career.[2] They have been characterized by a young medievalist who knows them well as the most distinguished bench of bishops in English history. Such a phrase is perhaps of conversational interest

[1] *L'Eglise et la royauté en Angleterre, 1154-89*, by Raymonde Foreville, Paris, 1943.

[2] The two other absentees are Robert of Bath and Walter of Rochester. For the complete list of bishops with dates, *see* Appendix I.

4

only, but if the estimate be restricted to the medieval centuries, one who challenges it will not find it easy to name a group to match that which contained, in addition to the great archbishop, such men as Gilbert Foliot, Henry of Blois, Robert of Melun, Bartholomew of Exeter, and Nigel of Ely. Moreover, the group has a collective significance in history in addition to the separate importance of individuals. On three decisive occasions at least—at Clarendon and Northampton in 1164, and for a third time in the autumn of 1169, the bishops were called upon as a body—at Clarendon in association with the archbishop, at Northampton and in 1169 in dissociation from him—to take their stand at a crisis of policy. Had they resolutely and unanimously opposed the king in 1164, or as unanimously fallen in with his wishes in 1169, the course of English church history would have been notably different.

It may be added that concentration on the actions and words of the archbishop alone, and the virtual relegation of his colleagues to the position of a chorus, if not of a conspiracy, has helped, in almost every recent account, to throw his figure out of historical perspective. It is only when we watch the attitude and consider the opinions of the other bishops, both before, during and after the great meetings of 1163-4, that we can see how many elements of the controversy, and how many of the views expressed, were the common property of all, or at least of most, of the school-trained ecclesiastics of the day, and how many were peculiar to Archbishop Thomas.

The task of narrating the actions and expounding the opinions and motives of the bishops as a group is simplified by two circumstances—the relatively small number of individuals with whom we have to deal, and the unusual length of the tenure of office of the majority among them.

Records would seem to show that bishops, outside times of persecution, are always good risks for the actuaries, but few groups of English bishops can have held their sees longer than those who lived through what seem to us in retrospect the exacting days of the anarchy under Stephen and the Becket controversy. Of the fifteen prelates who sat with Archbishop Thomas three held their sees for over forty years, four others for thirty or more, and yet another five for over twenty, the average length of rule for the fifteen men concerned being no less than twenty-eight years. We have to deal, therefore, in many cases with men long used to prelacy and with memories running far into the past. Moreover, between August, 1164, and the death of the archbishop in December, 1170—six-and-a-half years —no new appointments were made, though five bishops were removed by death, and we are in fact concerned with only a single bishop in each see between 1162 and 1170; for the apparent exception, Hereford, where the see changed hands during Archbishop Thomas's reign, finds compensation in London, whither Gilbert Foliot passed to fill an office which had for long lacked an effective holder. Such of the bishops as survived the crisis, therefore, had been present at its beginning. Clearly this circumstance makes the opinions and the actions of the group at once more significant and more readily ascertainable.

As has just been noted, we are concerned with fifteen prelates, two in the province of York (where the see of Carlisle was unoccupied between 1157 and 1189) and thirteen, excluding the archbishop, in that of Canterbury. They may be grouped in various ways for consideration, but before grouping them for more detailed treatment it will be well to consider how and when each of them attained his high office.

THE BISHOPS OF THE CONTROVERSY (1)

The *doyen* of the hierarchy in 1164, and perhaps also the oldest man among the bishops, was Henry of Winchester, King Stephen's brother and cousin of Henry II. His appointment, long ago in 1129, had been the direct act of Henry I, whose nephew he was.[1] Next in seniority, and possibly a few years older than Henry of Blois, came Nigel of Ely; he also dated from the reign of Henry I. Nephew (or son) of Roger of Salisbury and a cousin of Alexander the Magnificent of Lincoln, he was probably a royal treasurer when in 1131 he was appointed by the king to Ely.[2] These were the only two old Henricians, but eight dated from the reign of Stephen, and therefore owed their position to a more or less genuine form of canonical election or papal appointment.

The senior member of the group, Robert of Bath and Wells, was a Cluniac monk who owed his position entirely to Henry of Winchester;[3] next came Jocelin of Salisbury, whose election either by the chapter or by the legate had been a *pis aller*[4]; Hilary of Chichester, a bishop since 1147, was a papal nominee;[5] William Turbe of Norwich had been elected by his *confrères* of the priory there. Robert de Chesney of Lincoln had been the free

---

[1] *Annales Margan.*, *sub anno* 1129. 'Nepos regis Henricus nomine ex abbate Glastoniae rege iubente episcopus efficitur Wintonie.'

[2] Cf. the article by J. H. Round in *Dictionary of National Biography*, XLI.

[3] John of Worcester, 38. 'Sic . . . disposuit Wintoniensis episcopus Heinricus.'

[4] Cf. L. Voss, *Heinrich von Blois*, 42 *n.* 9, 44 *nn.* 18, 21, and *Gilberti Foliot*, ep. 11. A canonical election was nevertheless held; cf. J. A. Robinson, *Somerset Historical Essays*, 60.

[5] John of Hexham (Symeon of Durham), II 321.

canonical choice of his chapter.[1] Walter of Rochester, as was the custom with that semi-dependent see, was to all intents and purposes the nominee of the archbishop of Canterbury, who was in this case also his brother.[2] Hugh du Puiset of Durham, another nephew and candidate put forward by Henry of Winchester, had been freely elected by the monks of the cathedral priory.[3] Gilbert Foliot of Hereford, a Cluniac *confrère* of Henry of Winchester, owed his position directly to the influence of Archbishop Theobald,[4] as did also Roger of York, the archbishop's *protégé*, who was canonically elected by a well-canvassed chapter in the last months of Stephen's reign.[5] All these eight were thus men who in one way or another had been chosen by ecclesiastical agencies, at a time when the prestige, or at least the courage, of the Church was high in the reign of Stephen.

There remain the four appointments of the reign of Henry II. None of these took place until 1161, when Richard Peche was elected, probably canonically by one or both of his chapters, to the see of Coventry-Lichfield. A year later Bartholomew, another *protégé* of Theobald, was successfully proposed by the dying archbishop to king and chapter.[6] In the following year Gilbert Foliot was trans-

[1] *Gilberti Foliot, ep.* 88.

[2] An account of his election is in Gervase of Canterbury, I 132.

[3] John of Hexham (Symeon of Durham), II 328-9; Geoffrey of Coldingham, in *Historiae Dunelmensis Scriptores Tres* (Surtees Society vol. 9), ch. ii pp. 4-5. The election was formally 'free', but intrigues and threats had preceded it.

[4] John of Salisbury, *Historia Pontificalis*, xix (ed. Poole, p. 47).

[5] William of Newburgh, ed. Howlett (Rolls Series), ch. 26, 32, pp. 82, 95; cf. Guernes de Pont-Ste-Maxence, ed. Walberg, lines 267-9.

[6] John of Salisbury, *epp.* 80, 90.

lated to London by the Pope at the request of the king supported by his new archbishop of Canterbury,[1] and replaced at Hereford by the eminent Robert of Melun, *persona grata* with both Pope and archbishop.[2] Finally, in 1163 Roger, the king's cousin, was the archbishop's choice for Worcester.[3]

It will thus be seen that, with the exception of the two survivors from the days of Henry I, all the bishops were men who, to use the contemporary phrase, had entered the sheepfold by the door; that is, they owed their position, if not solely, at least primarily to merit in the service of the Church and to ecclesiastical rather than to royal initiative. The sole exception remains to be mentioned: it is Archbishop Thomas, whose election was the outcome of the king's *fiat* and was conducted, though perhaps not *contra*, yet at least *praeter voluntatem* as regards the original electors.

(iv)

We must now look a little more closely at the bishops, in order to consider their antecedents, characters and achievements. They fall into four groups: the royal officials; clerics who had risen through a regular career of church preferment; distinguished clerics who had risen to celebrity outside England; and, finally, the monks.

The first class contains strictly speaking only one member, Nigel of Ely, though of course Thomas of Canterbury himself belonged to it. Nigel of Ely, a Norman by birth, must have been a man well over sixty at Clarendon in 1163,

---

[1] *Materials for the History of Archbishop Thomas Becket*, V 24-30. Henceforward these will be cited as *Materials*.

[2] *Materials*, III 24, 260.

[3] *Materials*, III 259.

for as early as 1115 he was present on a public occasion
when Bishop Bernard of St David's made profession in the
royal presence. He need not detain us long, for he took no
prominent part in the great controversy, and died before
its *dénouement*.[1] He was in a sense an anachronism, a link
with the bad old days of his uncle Roger of Salisbury and
his cousin Alexander of Lincoln. Alone of Archbishop
Thomas's *confrères*, he had devoted all his energies and
abilities to matters purely secular; in the department of
financial administration he was supreme, and more than any
other man he helped to ensure the continuity and development of the excellent administrative practice initiated under
Henry I. This he did, possibly by his own work at the
Exchequer under Henry II, but more certainly by the
training and enthusiasm which passed from him to his son,
Richard Fitzneal, who became Treasurer at an uncertain
date early in the reign of Henry II and is celebrated as the
author of the classical handbook, the *Dialogus de Scaccario*,
in which he celebrates his father's genius in a series of
resounding phrases.[2] The mention of that son, who can

---

[1] For Nigel of Ely, Round's article, cited above, is still authorita-
tive, though much additional material has accumulated (see next
note). Nigel was at court in 1115, for he testifies to his presence
when Bernard, bishop of St David's, made his profession to Canterbury, *v.* J. Conway Davies, *Episcopal Acts relating to Welsh
Dioceses, 1066-1272,* I 264 D134.

[2] *Dialogus de Scaccario,* ed. Hughes, Crump and Johnson, pp.
96-7. 'Dominum Eliensem, virum . . . huius officii peritissimum,
cuius memoria in benedictione sit in eternum . . . Maximus autem
existens in his que ad sui status dignitatem pertinebant, celebrem sui
nominis famam fecit, adeo ut pene solus in regno sic vixerit et sic
decesserit ut gloriam eius invida lingua denigrare non audeat. Hic
etiam . . . scaccarii scientiam . . . pene prorsus abolitam reformauit,
et totius descriptionis eius formam velut alter Esdras bibliotece
sedulus reformator renovavit.' There has been much controversy

scarcely have been born of a legitimate union, is one more reminder that Nigel of Ely was not a high Gregorian; his career was not without vicissitudes; he took a leading part in the intrigues and combats of Stephen's reign, was besieged at Devizes and Ely and experienced a long series of adventures; his pride, wealth and military skill became the theme of chroniclers.[1] At various times he plundered the monks of Ely, who in return blackened his name and confused his story. Theobald is alleged to have written to him severely;[2] he was for a time suspended by his country-man Adrian IV, and some years later Archbishop Thomas took him to task.[3] As has been said, however, though he

---

as to whether Nigel was Treasurer under Henry I and Henry II; in the former case the affirmative, in the latter the negative decision seems probable. Cf. 'Richard Fitzneal and the *Dialogus de Scaccario*', by H. G. Richardson, in *Eng. Hist. Rev.*, XLIII 162, and the same writer's 'William of Ely, the King's Treasurer', in *Trans. Royal Hist. Soc.*, 4 ser., XV 46 *n*.1. References to the extensive literature will be found in both these papers. I owe these last references to Mr Brooke.

[1] *Gesta Stephani*, ed. Howlett (Rolls Series), 46, 49, 61-3; *Liber Eliensis*, passim, and J. H. Round, *Geoffrey de Mandeville*, 411-3.

[2] That is, if the address given by Giles for John of Salisbury's *ep.* 56 is correct. Round, however, in his notes on Nigel in *E.H.R.*, VIII (1893), 515-9, shows that he received permission from the Pope to be absent from the council of 1139, and the heading *Nigello* is a 14th century insertion in the MS used by Giles. (Cf. *E.H.R.* XXXVIII (1923), 558.) On the other hand, I cannot accept the opinion of W. Hunt, adopted by R. L. Poole (John of Salisbury, *Historia Pontificalis*, 110) that the letter was addressed to Foliot, who was present at the Lateran council of 1139 in a purely private capacity (cf. his letter to Brian fitzCount, *ep.* 79, ed. Giles, p. 100). Mr Brooke suggests that Robert Warelwast of Exeter alone suits all the requirements as addressee of the letter, and notes the confusion in the names of the bishops of Exeter in the *Handbook of British Chronology*.

[3] *Materials*, V 132-3.

stood with the rest against encroachment on clerical privileges he took little part in the main and deeper controversy. He was an ageing man in 1162; in 1163 he was incapacitated by a stroke and he died in 1169.[1]

The group of those who passed through the normal ecclesiastical career is more important. It includes the archbishop of York and the bishops of Durham, Coventry, Lincoln, Rochester, Salisbury and Worcester.

The archbishop of York, Roger of Pont l'Evêque, has been so severely handled by those who were his contemporaries that it is difficult to form a just estimate of his principles and sincerity. A Norman by birth, he was from early years a clerk in the household of Archbishop Theobald. There, when his career was still to make, he joined in a pact of mutual assistance (or log-rolling) with John Belmeis, later of Poitiers, and Thomas of London,[2] but he soon took a dislike, possibly deepened by a rival's jealousy, to his able and ambitious junior, whom he nicknamed derisively. Twice, we are told, he secured his dismissal, but Walter, the archbishop's brother and archdeacon, stood the young man's friend. When Walter became bishop of Rochester in 1148 Roger took his place as archdeacon. Although he was Theobald's official, he acted at Rome in 1152 on behalf of King Stephen against the policy of the archbishop. Despite this, his election to the see of York in 1154 was due to the direct action of Theobald, and according to William of Newburgh, no friend of Roger, was only achieved by threats and inten-

[1] Gervase of Canterbury, I 185, 'Ea tempestate' [*i.e.*, October, 1164] 'tactus est paralysi'.

[2] Will. Cant. in *Materials*, I 4. 'Cum eo [*sc.* Thoma] sociale foedus inierunt, condicentes ut in petendis sibi beneficiis ecclesiasticis suffragium suum communicarent ... Qui praesentes erant, pro se vel pro absentibus agebant.'

sive propaganda.[1] This favourable attitude of Theobald and the archbishop's confidence in him, as well as the friendship of Gilbert Foliot, must stand on the credit side of his account. On the debit side there has been set a letter, sometimes erroneously cited as by John of Salisbury,[2] in which the clerks of Archbishop Thomas, writing in 1171-2 with an abusive letter of Roger's before them, bring up against him a charge of unnatural vice, dating from old days at Canterbury. The charge is circumstantial, with references to a compurgation before Theobald in which Thomas is said to have taken a complaisant part, and to a further defence at Rome. Roger was certainly out at Rome at a date which would fit the reference, but his business, so it appears, was different. Both the letter of the clerks and that of Roger[3] have aroused the suspicions of a great

[1] v. supra, p. 8, note 5.

[2] *Materials*, VII 525-9. This, in Giles's edition, bears the address *Willelmo Senonensi archiepiscopo Joannes Saresberiensis*, but it is ostensibly written by *miseri illi qui quondam fuere Cantuarienses*, and there is nothing to suggest John's authorship. The long and abusive passage is not in his manner. Mr Brooke adds: 'From my father's notes, I gather that this letter is in Vat. Lat. 1220 (Bk v, No. 91) and Cott. Claudius B II (V No. 97). It follows one of John to the archbishop of Sens, and in the index to Vat. Lat. 1220 it is called "idem ad eundem". It is clearly an error in rubrication; cf. my father's note: "The rubricator of these indices made several mistakes" '.

[3] *Materials*, VII 504-6 (Dec., 1171). R. L. Poole, in his note 'Two documents concerning archbishop Roger of York', in *Speculum* III (1928), 81-4 (reprinted in *Studies in Chronology and History* (ed. A. L. Poole), 298-301) suggested that the most abusive part of this letter was an interpolation, but gave no positive proof for his suspicion. Roger's statement that his enemies had visited the Curia *cum meretricibus suis*, which Poole considered evidence of fabrication, might surely in the rather intemperate context be taken to refer simply to the presence of some of the exiled relatives or dependents of Archbishop Thomas.

scholar of our own day,[1] and in view of the high opinion held of Roger by both Theobald and Gilbert Foliot,[2] and the absence of any contemporary references to his alleged judicial difficulties, it would be rash to attach any weight whatever to the precise charge of immorality made by the clerks.

As archbishop, he pressed his claims and authority in every direction: to consecrate the archbishop of Canterbury; to carry his cross in the southern province; to crown kings. When once he, *malorum omnium incentor et caput*,[3] had been won over by Henry II, in pursuance of Arnulf's advice to split the opposition, he became the archbishop's most relentless enemy. The biographers of St Thomas are, as is natural, unanimous in their abuse, and it is unfortunate that the independent if somewhat deceptively critical William of Newburgh should have been Roger's implacable enemy owing to a collision between the archbishop and the canons of the chronicler's own house. The evidence of records shows the archbishop as a benefactor to other religious houses and as a builder of magnificence. He was extremely wealthy, and neither his letters nor his recorded acts show the least trace of any spiritual feeling.

Hugh du Puiset, the long-lived, powerful and opulent

---

[1] R. L. Poole in the article cited.

[2] *Gilberti Foliot ep.* 17 (=97) to Eugenius III (this is probably a Gloucester letter written before Roger was archdeacon, *i.e.*, before 1148): 'Clericus enim dilecti filii vestri domini Cantuariensis archiepiscopi, magister Rogerus de Ponte episcopi, vestrum adiit urgente necessitate presidium ad tuenda ea quae canonice possidet a vestra implorat serenitate patrocinium'. Roger is referred to as: 'tam vita quam scientia dignum'.

[3] Archbishop Thomas to Alexander III (late 1170) in *Materials*, VII 387.

bishop of Durham, though one of the most vigorous holders of a see distinguished by the fighting spirit of its occupants, need not detain us, since for reasons which do not appear he kept entirely clear of the controversy and was present neither at Clarendon nor at Northampton.[1] We may merely note in passing that he was one of the numerous nephews whose interests were furthered by their uncle, Henry of Blois, and that he had in early life been clerk and later archdeacon to his uncle at Winchester.

Nor need we delay over Richard Peche, bishop of Lichfield and Coventry, the son of Robert Peche, a previous holder of the see. He was present at Clarendon, but neither there nor later, with the exception of an occasion to be mentioned in its place, did he show any individuality of word or act.

Robert de Chesney, bishop of Lincoln, was not one of the chief actors in the struggle, though his name appears from time to time, nor is he among the most distinguished holders of his see, but he is of interest as showing the inter-relation of the Norman families from which the higher ecclesiastics sprang. He was an English-born scion of the Norman family of Cheyney or Chesney, deriving from Quesnay between St Lô and Caen.[2] The head of the English clan was Ralf, who came over towards the end of the eleventh century and obtained lands near Bosham in

[1] The best account of Bishop Hugh is still that of Stubbs, in his preface to the third volume of Roger of Hoveden's chronicle (Rolls Series, 51), pp. xxxiii–xxxvii.

[2] For the Chesney family see H. E. Salter, *Chartulary of Eynsham Abbey* (Oxford Historical Society, XLIX), pp. 411-23; W. Farrer, *Honors and Knights' Fees*. III 227; L. F. Salzman, 'Sussex Domesday Tenants. IV. The Family of Chesney', in *Sussex Archaeological Collections* LXV (1924), 20 ff.

Sussex and elsewhere. While part of the family retained its Sussex home, a son, Roger, planted a new offshoot in Oxfordshire, and by his marriage with Aliz de Langetot became father of a large family of at least nine children, one of whom was the future bishop of Lincoln. One of his daughters, of whom there is no record, must have married a Foliot, for Gilbert Foliot more than once unequivocally refers to the bishop as his uncle.[1] Robert de Chesney took to the Church and rose to be archdeacon of Leicester, whence he was canonically elected to succeed Alexander the Magnificent in 1148. Gilbert Foliot wrote warmly to the Pope in support of his candidature, and in the years that followed is constantly found in correspondence with him, using terms of affection which suggest a warmer feeling than the conventional respect due to an elder relative.[2] Like Roger of York and his own predecessor Alexander, Bishop Robert was a builder of episcopal palaces, but so far as the indications of chroniclers go, supported as they are by his recorded words and actions, he was not a man of strong character or decided opinions.[3] He died at the end of 1166.

The bishop of Rochester, Walter, was, as has been

[1] Gilbert Foliot in *ep.* 54 refers to William de Chesney as his *avunculus*. In *ep.* 221, in which William de Chesney was alluded to as the bishop's brother, Foliot intercedes for his own *nepos* who is the bishop's *abnepos*. The chronicler of St Albans mentions the relationship (*Gesta Abbatum S. Albani*, I 139).

[2] Cf. *ep.* 90: 'carissime'; *ep.* 128: ... 'ut optatos occuramus in amplexus ... valeat dominus meus et frater in Christo carissimus'. Cf. *ep.* 143.

[3] The biographers of Archbishop Thomas allude to Robert as *simplex* and *humilis*. He died in debt to the Jewish financier, Aaron of Lincoln (Giraldus Cambrensis, *Opera*, VI 36).

mentioned, the brother of Archbishop Theobald; he was therefore a Norman clerk who owed his residence in England and his career to his brother. Theobald made him archdeacon—a post very often given to a near relative— and later appointed him bishop of Rochester. This, the smallest and least important of the English sees, excluding Carlisle, had long stood in a relationship of peculiar dependence upon the metropolitan. Its occupant was, even after the Lateran decrees of 1139, recognized by Alexander III himself as a pure nominee of the archbishop, even if a formal consent may have been given to the appointment by the Rochester community in the chapter-house of Canterbury; very often, indeed, he was a monk of one or other of the houses. He was regarded as a kind of super-chaplain to the archbishop, and in his absence often administered the archdiocese. Walter has the distinction of having occupied the see for thirty-four years, a longer space than any other bishop from the Conquest to the present day, longer even than Hamo de Hethe or John Fisher; but in ability he was no rival to Theobald. As archdeacon he had been on two critical occasions the patron of Thomas of London, and the great archbishop used him on more than one occasion as a personal envoy whom he could employ as a matter of course. Yet though bound so closely to the church of Canterbury by antecedents and tradition, he was by no means conspicuously loyal to his exiled metropolitan or vigorous in his defence.

The bishop of Salisbury, Jocelin de Bohun, was destined to play an important, if not very glorious, part in the long series of disputes. The problem of his parentage has taxed the ingenuity and learning of a succession of antiquaries and scholars, including Stubbs, Round, R. L. Poole, the late L. C. Loyd and the present President of St John's

College, Oxford; it still remains obscure.[1] The family of
Bohun derived from S. Georges de Bohon near Carentan,
in the modern department of Manche. The name of
Jocelin's father is not known, but the bishop was, according
to William FitzStephen, a nephew of Engelger de Bohun,
the son of Richard de Meri; he thus belonged to the branch
of the family later established near Midhurst rather than to
that whence sprang the Earls of Hereford. He was related
in some way not yet traceable to the Earls of Gloucester,
and he was probably a first cousin once removed of the
well-connected if slightly elusive Savaric, bishop of Bath
and Wells at the end of the century.[2] His brother Richard

---

[1] The Bohun genealogy presents many problems, some of which
have yet to be solved. The conclusions of Stubbs (preface to
Epistolae Cantuarienses, Rolls Series) were invalidated on important
points by the French charters published by Round in *Calendar of
Documents preserved in France*, 669, 1213, 1215; cf. introd. p. xlv
et seqq. Since then others, and in particular the late L. C. Loyd and
A. L. Poole (*Essays presented to R. L. Poole*, pp. 264ff), have devoted
much time and scholarship to the Bohun pedigree. I have to thank
the President of St. John's College, Oxford (Mr A. L. Poole) for
communicating some of his notes to me; Mr C. T. Clay, who
informed me of the whereabouts of Loyd's notes; and Professor
D. C. Douglas, who allowed me to see the genealogical tree of the
Bohuns which Loyd drew up. Most unfortunately, no documentary
material has come to light which might enable us to fix with precision the place of Jocelin and his brother. In Loyd's tree he was
originally inserted as the son of an unrecorded brother of Engelger
(Enjuger), but for an unexplained reason Loyd on second thoughts
cancelled his name there without inserting it at any other point. We
are thus left completely in the dark. In the past, there had been a
curious confusion of Jocelin de Bohun with Jocelin de Baileul, a
king's clerk who often appears as witness of charters, sometimes
along with his namesake. For Jocelin's pedigree, v. Appendix II.

[2] That would be the relationship if it were accepted that Jocelin
was a nephew of Engelger and that Savaric was a grandson of

18

became bishop of Coutances. Jocelin had a son, Reginald
FitzJocelin, known as the Lombard from the country in
which his youth had been spent and in which, perhaps, he
had been born. Reginald was twenty-three in 1174,[1] which
would just permit of the hypothesis, cherished by more
than one genealogist, of his legitimate birth accompanied
or closely followed by the death of his mother, and Reginald
did in fact adduce some very cautiously worded evidence
in 1174 that he had been begotten before his father was
ordained priest,[2] but the uncompromising reference by
Archbishop Thomas to 'that bastard son of a priest, born
of a harlot' would seem conclusive evidence against
legitimacy, for all its somewhat intemperate context.[3] The
bishop was devoted to his son, whom he made his archdeacon and who gave him loyal support in his troubles,
and one writer, noting Reginald's recurring visits to
S. Jean de Maurienne, has found a mother for him in the
noble family of Maurienne, which would bring him into
relationship with the house of Burgundy and the Emperor
Henry VI. This is as it may be. What is certain is that
Jocelin, somewhat unexpectedly, was claimed as a personal
friend of olden days by Alexander III, who had been the

Muriel, sister or half-sister of Engelger. But, as mentioned in the
previous note, Jocelin's pedigree is very uncertain. It may be noted
that Robert, Earl of Gloucester, was a patron of Jocelin, and that
Earl William of Gloucester refers to the bishop as *cognatus suus*
(charter to Tewkesbury in Dugdale, *Monasticon*, II 74).

[1] Wharton, *Anglia Sacra*, I 561.

[2] Rad. de Diceto (Rolls Series), I 391: 'Alii juraverunt quod,
sicut opinabantur, conceptus fuit priusquam Jocelinus pater suus
ad gradum sacerdotii promoveretur'.

[3] *Materials*, VII 181 (Archbishop Thomas to his agents): 'Illum
spurium, fornicarium . . . sacerdotis filium'. It may be remarked
that Jocelin, as archdeacon, was probably only in deacon's orders
when elected bishop.

great canonist Rolando Bandinelli,[1] and this suggests further interesting but fruitless speculation as to the bishop's early life and studies. Such of his letters as survive, it must be confessed, give little evidence of either mental power or legal lore sufficient to have made him a favourite pupil of Master Roland.

Jocelin was another of Henry of Winchester's young men, and he became in due course archdeacon of Winchester. His further promotion was on a side wind in 1142. Stephen had refused the candidate put forward by the bishop of Winchester—yet one more of his nephews, Henry de Sully; whereupon the legate had in turn blocked the king's choice, his chancellor, Philip de Harcourt. Finally, after administering or neglecting the see for some time, Henry as legate acquiesced in the appointment of his archdeacon, patronized by Robert, Earl of Gloucester, whose kinsman he was, and who was a supporter of the Empress, who at that time controlled Wiltshire.

As bishop, Jocelin had frequent contact with Gilbert Foliot, then abbot of Gloucester; the vexatious affair of Cernel, in particular, which occurred within the diocese of Salisbury, brought them often together; but Foliot's early letters show not merely a formal respect but a real measure of friendship.[2] When Foliot himself became bishop the exchange of letters ceases, possibly because the two now met regularly at royal councils and elsewhere, but the old

[1] *Materials*, VI 568: 'Qualiter jampridem venerabilem fratrem nostrum Jocelinum ... dilexerimus et quanta ipse devotione ac familiaritate etiam ante nostrae promotionis initia nobis adstrictius adhaeserit, et nos bene recolimus', &c.

[2] Cf. *ep.* 11 to Lucius III, where Foliot refers to him as: 'antistitem vitae commendabilis et gratiae ... qui ante vocationem suam studiis honestatis incessanter incubuit'. Foliot here alludes to the first words of the account of St Benedict by Gregory the Great.

familiarity between the two men of the same social class was to have its consequences.

At some time during the early years of Henry II Jocelin fell heavily under the king's displeasure,[1] and it is possible that the Sarum charters tell us a part, at least, of the story.[2] From them we learn that Pope Eugenius III compelled the Empress to restore Bishop's Cannings and Potterne to Salisbury in 1148, and that the transaction was completed in 1149 by Henry, then Duke of Normandy. In 1152 Henry II took the castle of Devizes from Jocelin for three years, and in 1157 the bishop was forced to release it to the king in permanence in exchange for some other land and for a charge of £30 *per annum* on Godalming, a sheriff's payment that can be traced year by year in the Pipe Rolls.[3] This may have been the transaction which Archbishop Thomas

---

[1] References to this offence are common in the biographies of Archbishop Thomas, though it is nowhere specified by them. The only clue is given by the archbishop (*Materials*, VII 241) when he reminds the Pope that Jocelin lost Devizes and many other possessions: 'quia ipsum [*sc.* regem] ad faciendam restitutionem, juramenti religione arctatum decessorum vestrorum Anastasii et Adriani litteris, ausus est convenire'. These letters are not calendared in Jaffé-Loewenfeld. Alexander III also alludes to Jocelin's troubles when he speaks of his own request to Thomas, then presumably chancellor, to use his good offices to effect a reconciliation between Jocelin and Henry, which he had in fact successfully done. Jocelin, it may be added, awoke the memory of old offences by supporting Archbishop Thomas in his assertion of the rights of clerical offenders (Herbert of Bosham in *Materials*, III).

[2] Cf. *Charters and Documents of Salisbury* (Rolls Series), ed. W. Rich-Jones and W. D. Macray, Nos. xv, xvii, xxv, xxxv.

[3] The payment by the sheriff of £30 from Godalming *pro Escambia de Divisis* appears in every Pipe Roll from 1158-9 to 1169-70; I did not pursue it further.

later described as the penalty for obedience to Rome,[1] but it does not fully account for the king's lasting hostility.

Jocelin's character, as seen in his letters and actions, is that of a somewhat irresolute man, turning for support and guidance now to the archbishop, now to Foliot, and now to the king. There is in him something of the Gloucester in *King Lear*. In addition, some of his letters and recorded utterances have a ring of a somewhat ponderous jocularity.[2]

With Roger of Worcester we touch another type and another generation. The younger son of Robert, Earl of Gloucester, the illegitimate son of Henry I, and thus a cousin of Henry II, Roger was for a time educated at Bristol with the future king,[3] and later studied at Paris under Robert de Melun. When still young, he was appointed to the see of Worcester in 1163, but though he no doubt owed his early promotion to his cousin, he was already, and he remained, on terms of peculiar friendship with his consecrator, the archbishop, who often reminded him of the link between them; he was in fact the most loyal as he was also the most courageous and perhaps also the most spiritual of Thomas's colleagues, despite an occasional

[1] After the archbishop had gone into exile, Henry distrained Jocelin for the sums for which he had gone surety on behalf of Thomas; cf. *Materials*, V 223 (John of Poitiers to Thomas): 'Dominum Saresberiensem in tantum praegravasse dicitur rex, ut nec uno bove hodie dominium ecclesiae Saresberiensis excolatur'.

[2] E.g., *Materials*, VI 267-8.

[3] Cf. the words of Henry to Roger of Worcester at Falaise in 1170, referring to Robert of Gloucester: 'qui me et te in castro illo [*sc.* Bristol] nutrivit et nos ibi et prima elementa morum et litterarum doceri procuravit' (William FitzStephen in *Materials*, III 104). Roger was later the pupil of Robert of Melun. For Robert, Earl of Gloucester, *v.* G. H. White, 'The illegitimate children of Henry I', Appendix D to vol. XI of *The Complete Peerage*.

sally at the archbishop's expense.[1] Gerald of Wales selected him as one of the outstandingly able and exemplary English bishops of his time, and in a well known passage tells us that Alexander III referred to him and the bishop of Exeter as the two great luminaries of the English church.[2]

[1] *Materials*, VI 321 (John of Salisbury to Bartholomew of Exeter): 'Wigorniensis qui, si vera sunt quae dicuntur, plus quam tantae modestiae virum deceat in archiepiscopum suum jocatus est'.

[2] Giraldus Cambrensis, *Opera*, VII 57. 'Erant enim quasi gemina candelabra . . . Unde et papa Alexander tertius duo magna luminaria Anglicanae ecclesiae dicebat hos esse.'

CHAPTER II

THE BISHOPS OF THE CONTROVERSY (2)

(i)

THREE other secular bishops remain, distinguished from those just mentioned by the fact that their reputation had been chiefly made outside England. These are Hilary of Chichester, Bartholomew of Exeter and Robert of Hereford.

The personality of Hilary of Chichester impresses itself sharply if not very pleasantly upon every student of the age. Originally a clerk in the household of Henry of Winchester, he was in due course appointed dean of the secular college of Twyneham, later Christchurch, in Hampshire.[1] At some unspecified date he found his way to the Curia, where he soon made for himself a reputation as counsel and advocate in cases heard before the Pope.[2] He was successful in impressing even Eugenius III while remaining in favour with King Stephen, and when in 1147 William of York was deposed, he was the king's candidate for the vacant see and apparently obtained a majority of the suffrages. Another party, however, including the two suffragans of Durham and Carlisle, supported the Cister-

---

[1] Some of the facts about Hilary are in the *Dict. Nat. Biog.* and in an article by J. H. Round in the *Athenaeum* of January 23rd, 1897: Brian fitzCount in a letter of 1142 (*E.H.R.* XXV (1910), 302) refers to: 'Hylarium decanum de Christeschire (*sic*)'; in 1145 he was present at Rochester with the legate Imar (Thorpe, *Registrum Roffense*, 42).

[2] John of Hexham (Symeon of Durham), II 321: 'Qui Hylarius in ministerio Henrici Wintoniae episcopi plurimum gloriae pretium emeruit. Postea ad ministerium Apostolici translatus, in reddendis et prosequendis causis advocatus disertissimus et juris consulti peritus in curia Romana fuit'.

cian, Henry Murdac, and when the matter was referred to the Pope Eugenius appointed the abbot of Fountains, while praising the bishop-elect,[1] and within a few days placed Hilary in the see of Chichester, regarded as vacant through the deposition in 1145, for reasons not known to us, of Seffrid, who survived till 1151.[2] Henceforward Hilary's name is constantly recurring, almost always in incidents that illuminate his character and talents. In 1148 he was one of the three bishops sent to the council of Rheims by Stephen to excuse the absence of Theobald, who had been forbidden to go, but who nevertheless escaped from England and appeared in person.[3] In the same year, he was ordered by the Pope to consecrate Gilbert Foliot, newly elected to Hereford and still the friend of the Empress. Hilary refused, alleging that it was contrary to the customs of the realm to consecrate a bishop abroad who had not yet received the king's approval.[4] In his diocese he appears some years later endeavouring to reduce to normal canonical submission the abbey of Battle, which enjoyed the exempt status of royal *eigen-kloster*. His tactless and provocative exposition of papal claims ultimately brought down on him the wrath of the king, after which his recantation and submission were as complete as could be desired.[5]

---

[1] John of Hexham, *loc. cit.* 'Cum plurima tamen electae personae commendatione.'

[2] Henry of Huntingdon (316) records his deposition in 1147; cf. also F. Liebermann, *Ungedruckte Geschichtsquellen*, 95, where the year 1145 is given.

[3] John of Salisbury, *Historia Pontificalis*, ii, pp. 7-8. Gervase of Canterbury, I 138, is probably in error.

[4] John of Salisbury, *op. cit.*, xix, 47.

[5] *Chronicon Monasterii de Bello* (Anglia Christiana Society), 90 et seqq.

Hilary was regarded by his brother bishops, and in particular by Theobald, as an authority on canon law, and in Theobald's letters he figures some ten times (more than twice as frequently as any other bishop) as one of the assessors of the archbishop in a difficult case, and he was often employed as a papal judge-delegate. At Chichester he was energetic in organizing the personnel and finances of his household and church; the treasury was established with an income within a year of his consecration,[1] and the chancery put on its feet a few years later.[2] It is surely no coincidence that three of the learned clerks of Archbishop Thomas's *familia* came from Chichester:[3] they were no doubt Hilary's young men, as may also have been Herbert of Bosham.

Hilary was one of the three bishops sent from Normandy in May, 1162, to effect the election of the chancellor to the archbishopric. There was a considerable amount of demur and heart-searching, both at Canterbury and Westminster, and Gilbert Foliot is said to have attempted, by an expedient not unknown to boards and councils, to shelve an unpalatable decision by proposing that the matter, as a controversial one, should rest unsettled till the king had given it further attention. Hilary immediately countered this by remarking that the intentions of the king were known as fully as could be desired.[4] When an abbot present brought forward once

---

[1] The bull of Eugenius III is dated from Rheims, April 18th, 1148 (Holtzmann, *Papsturkunden in England*, II 57). It is a bull of protection, in which the treasury is mentioned as already established.

[2] Alexander III, June 4th, 1163, in renewing protection, adds the chancery (Holtzmann, *op. cit.*, II 113).

[3] *Sc.*, Jordan of Melbourne, then archdeacon and later dean of Chichester; Matthew of Chichester, likewise later dean; Gervase of Chichester (Herbert of Bosham in *Materiais*, III 526-7).

[4] *Thomas Saga*, I 74

more the argument that a monk would be the fittest occupant of the chair of Augustine, Hilary dealt with him summarily by asking if he thought that only one of his way of life could be pleasing to God.

From all these incidents, and from those that follow in the course of the struggle, an impression of the bishop of Chichester emerges so consistent and so clear that it can scarcely be a mistaken one. He appears as an extremely quick-witted, efficient, self-confident, voluble, somewhat shallow man, fully acquainted with the new canon law, but not prepared to abide by principles to the end. His talents were great, but he used them as an opportunist. Though capable of extremes of tactless display, he was a useful ally by reason of his nimble mind and lack of delicacy. He was at his strongest when acting as the agent of an authority in the ascendant, and he was never reluctant to transfer his services from one power to another more effective or more immediate.

With Bartholomew of Exeter we come to one of the most distinguished of the bishops. His career and work have in recent years been the subject of an able study,[1] and there is therefore less need here to stress his significance. In origin a Norman of the diocese of Coutances, it is probable that he studied at Paris, and he was a master of distinction there *circa* 1140-2, when he would have been somewhat over thirty years old. A single but precise reference seems to make it certain that he had been for a time a member of the archbishop's household,[2] and this would explain the growth of the intimate friendship that

[1] *Bartholomew of Exeter*, by Dom Adrian Morey (Cambridge, 1937).

[2] *Materials*, I 407: 'Pater noster Bartholomaeus, Cantuariensis ecclesiae alumnus'.

existed between Bartholomew and John of Salisbury; he would also have known well, both as colleagues and archdeacons, the two future archbishops, Roger and Thomas. He himself became archdeacon of Exeter in 1155, and in 1159, as an expert canonist, took part in the deliberations of the London synod convoked to decide upon the claims of the rivals for the papacy, Victor IV and Alexander III; he was subsequently sent by Theobald to the king with the verdict of the assembly. Exeter fell vacant in March, 1160, and the last months of Theobald's life were troubled by his anxiety to secure the post for Bartholomew, of whom he wrote in the most laudatory terms, as against an unworthy candidate favoured by the king.[1] John of Salisbury was, throughout the long negotiations, a friendly and helpful correspondent. Theobald achieved his end before his death, but did not live to consecrate the elect. Within a few months we find Bartholomew employed by the king as one of the envoys sent to arrange the election of the chancellor at Canterbury and Westminster.

Bartholomew was a trained theologian and canonist, and several of his works are extant, including the penitential, printed by Dom Morey, which had a considerable vogue at the time. He was also, more than any other English bishop, employed in his later years as a judge-delegate. Though only a few of the letters written to him by John of Salisbury survive, they, and the letters addressed by John to Baldwin, archdeacon of Exeter, are evidence of the respectful affection with which Bartholomew was regarded —a respect with which Archbishop Thomas fully concurred.

Of all the English bishops of his day Robert of Hereford

---

[1] Cf. letters of Theobald and John of Salisbury to Thomas, *Materials*, V 12, 14.

had perhaps the highest reputation on the Continent.[1] Born in England, probably before 1100 as he was an old man at the time of his election to Hereford, he went to France early in the century and was the pupil in turn of Hugh of St Victor and Abelard. He himself taught on the Mont Ste Geneviève after Abelard's departure, and subsequently settled at Melun, where he had among his pupils John of Salisbury, Thomas of London, later archbishop, and Roger of Worcester.[2] Herbert of Bosham, writing after the chequered pattern of the controversy had unfolded, still speaks of him as a luminary whose light shone throughout the world, sending out from himself his pupils as rays to the uttermost parts, and remarks that his character was as distinguished as his learning. Shortly before Robert's return to England, John of Salisbury, also, had written words of high praise; if Robert and his other master, Alberic, could have been thrown into one, he said, the age would not have seen their equal.[3] Later, as we shall see, John was considerably less complimentary, and the change in estimation consequent upon a cooling of friendly relations is a noteworthy fact which should be borne in mind when considering John's judgment of others. Robert of Melun's chief work was his *Liber Sententiarum* or *Summa Theologica*, celebrated in its day, which, in the eyes of that eminent historian of scholastic method, Mgr Grabmann, is an important link in the history of theology between the methods of Abelard and Hugh of St Victor and the epoch-

---

[1] For Robert of Melun, *v.* Ueberweg-Geyer, *Grundriss der Geschichte der Philosophie* (1928), II 276-8.

[2] Herbert of Bosham in *Materials*, III 260. 'Cujus et ille sacerdos magnus . . . in scholis discipulus fuerat.'

[3] For John's praise of Robert *v. Metalogicon* (ed. Webb) bk. ii, ch. 10, p. 79.

making Book of the Sentences of Peter the Lombard.[1] Robert of Melun knew the Lombard well, and was associated with him in opposition to Gilbert de la Porrée at Rheims in 1148. In 1163 he was in England, and was one of those sent to persuade the archbishop to accept the royal customs. At almost the same time, he was warmly recommended by Thomas for the vacancy at Hereford, and was consecrated to that see by the archbishop on the feast of St Thomas, 1163.[2]

There remains the third group, that of the monks. Monastic members of the hierarchy between the Conquest and the reign of John were repeatedly men of such eminent administrative or spiritual gifts—and not infrequently of both together: we think of a Wulfstan, a Lanfranc, a Gundulf, a William of St Calais, an Anselm, a Theobald, a Henry Murdac, a Hugh of Lincoln—that it is very easy to receive the impression that they were numerically a stronger body than was in fact the case. Actually, for the century and a half after the Conquest, the number of monk-bishops in office rarely exceeded three or four and sank at times to zero; there is in this respect, therefore, nothing exceptional in their strength during the Becket controversy. But as on other occasions, so here: among the monk-bishops were the men who were the most outstanding and influential members of their body: both Henry of Winchester and Gilbert Foliot were in 1162, and had long been, the most distinguished churchmen in the country, equalling, and at times, at least in the case of Henry, appearing to surpass, Theobald himself in ability and in repute.

One of these monks, Robert of Bath and Wells, need not detain us. A Cluniac of Lewes, he had been introduced

---

[1] M. Grabmann, *Geschichte der scholastischen Methode*, II 354.
[2] Gervase of Canterbury, I 176.

at St Swithun's, Winchester, as cathedral prior soon after the accession of Henry of Blois; he was soon entrusted by the bishop with the administration of Glastonbury, which Henry continued to rule so far as title went till the end of his life, and finally, by the same agency, he was elected bishop of Bath, where he did much to regularize the relations of the see both with Wells and with Glastonbury; he took a leading part in establishing the chapter at Wells, and both there and at Bath building was in progress in his day.[1] Though he must have been a man of considerable parts to pass so quickly from one position of trust to another, he must also have been an old man by 1162; his last recorded appearance was at the consecration of the new archbishop.[2] He may have become almost immediately after this an invalid or an imbecile, for it is recorded that illness prevented him in May, 1163, from attending the council of Tours. In any case his name, unique in this respect among the English bishops, does not once occur in the voluminous Becket material.

William of Norwich was the only English black monk of the four. Born probably before 1100, he had been among the early generations of the children of the cloister at the cathedral priory of Norwich, recently founded by Bishop Herbert de Losinga, whose conversion from simony and avarice is characterized by William of Malmesbury as epoch-making: *momentum et mutatio rerum*.[3] The young

[1] J. Armitage Robinson, *Somerset Historical Essays*, 55-62.

[2] Robert's last appearance in public would seem to have been at Archbishop Thomas's consecration (Gervase of Canterbury, I 171). For his illness in May, 1163, v. Rad. de Diceto (Rolls Series), I 310.

[3] For William v. E. M. Goulburn and H. Symons, *Life and Letters and Sermons of Herbert Losinga* (Oxford, 2 vols.,1878), letters xli, xlii, xlii (bis). Cf. also A. Jessop and M. R. James, *St William of Norwich*, xix, xxi, *et seqq.*, and the article by Jessop in *Dict. Nat. Biog.* Malmesbury's allusion (*Gesta Regum*, II 386-7) is to Lucan,*Pharsalia*,IV 819.

William was one of the bishop's especial *protégés*, and letters exist in which he encourages and exhorts him to study, and affectionately warns him of his impetuous character. Soon after Losinga's death William appears as subprior and prior of the house, and in the latter capacity distinguished himself by the energy with which he bore down all opposition to the cult of the alleged child-martyr, William of Norwich. While the domestic controversy concerning the merits of the young victim was still fierce, William was elected by his brethren bishop of Norwich, and was able to secure the acceptance of St William as the occupant of the tutelary shrine of the cathedral. William was a man of learning, in the monastic literary tradition, with an especial fluency in verse. As an English monk elected by his brethren he stood apart at once from the clerks of the career, and from the relatives and young men of Henry of Winchester. William does not appear as a correspondent of Gilbert Foliot in the early years, possibly because his diocese was so far removed from Foliot's sphere, but later the bishop of London writes to the Pope in the warmest, almost effusively affectionate, terms of him as 'his own most dear and venerable brother, whose life from childhood to old age has been one long exhibition of worth, and who has been an ornament of the Church from the cradle'.[1] That William himself could admire and love worth in others is seen from an affectionate letter written to Gilbert of Sempringham, his *alter ego*, when the founder was in trouble.[2] The bishop of Norwich must indeed, as an

[1] *Materials*, VI 292-3: 'Venerabilis et carissimi fratris nostri . . . praeclara ab ineunte aetate usque in senectutem bonam merita . . . ab ipsis fere cunabulis per omnes aetatum gradus honeste conversatum.'

[2] D. Knowles, 'The Revolt of the Lay Brothers of Sempringham', in *E.H.R.* L (1935), 479-80.

old man, have been regarded with a kind of filial affection by those of his colleagues capable of such a feeling, for the exiled archbishop, when on the point of returning in 1170, prays with prophetic solemnity that his eyes may see Bishop William before the writer dies, while a few days later, reversing the prayer, he hopes to see the bishop before the latter takes flight to eternity.[1] John of Salisbury, likewise, in the days of the exile, writes always in terms of affectionate reverence. William of Norwich won this respect by his firmness as well as by his benignity; in 1156 he was one of the leaders in the opposition to scutage,[2] and it was possibly the memory of Henry's anger on that occasion that led him, at a critical moment at Clarendon, to plead with the archbishop to give way, since the safety of his colleagues was at stake also. It is not the part which we should have expected him to play, but he is recorded as wishing in 1164 that he too, like Nigel of Ely, were sick of the palsy.[3]

(ii)

We have now to confront the two most remarkable personalities among the colleagues of Archbishop Thomas. Both were men of high—one, indeed, was of the highest—social rank; both had been as young men monks at the magnificent abbey of Cluny; and both had been, for a quarter of a century and more, in high place. While it is not certain that either had passed through the schools of Bologna, both had what has sometimes been called the high

---

[1] *Materials*, VII 344, 416.

[2] John of Salisbury (writing for Theobald), *ep.* 128.

[3] Gervase of Canterbury, I 185: 'Ea tempestate [*sc.* January, 1164] Willelmus Norvicensis excusavit se, secreto asserens Elyensem feliciter a Deo defensum, et quod ipse vellet simili plaga percelli'.

Gregorian attitude towards matters of church polity and practice: they held, that is, that the clerical body should form a class apart from the laity, governed by its own laws, amenable only to its own courts, compactly organized upon its pivot, the papacy, whence through decrees, legates and judges-delegate it would receive constant direction. But though their social and religious background was similar and though their outlook on the external activities of religion was taken from the same standpoint, there was, it would seem, little intimacy between them. Foliot's letters to the bishop of Winchester are few and formal, and the two men scarcely ever consulted, or collaborated with, each other.[1]

Henry of Blois, younger brother of King Stephen, and thus nephew of Henry I and cousin of Henry II, was in many ways a very remarkable man. As a king-maker he has only one rival in English history, as a bishop he has been hailed by an eminent scholar as the greatest uncanonized English prelate of his century,[2] and as a supremely able financier and administrator he manifested in one theatre after another the genius of a Woolton or a Keynes, while as a connoisseur and collector of antiques he was without a rival in his age. Appointed by a royal act of power to the abbey of Glastonbury in his twenties, and to the wealthy bishopric of Winchester when he was thirty, he was for some eight years (1135-43), during four of which he was

---

[1] In what follows I have used the materials collected for the section on the two eminent Cluniacs in *The Monastic Order in England*, ch. xvi. There is a good monograph by Dr Lena Voss on *Heinrich von Blois* (Berlin, 1932). Gilbert Foliot still awaits the study which Dom Adrian Morey and Mr C. N. L. Brooke are carrying to completion.

[2] Edmund Bishop, *Liturgica Historica* (Oxford, 1918), 394.

papal legate with precedence over the archbishop of Canterbury, unquestionably the most powerful agency both in secular and in ecclesiastical politics, which indeed became inextricably mingled in his hands. While holding high Gregorian views as to the centralization of the Church and the paramountcy of the spiritual power, he nevertheless used every opportunity and all his influence to promote relatives and *protégés* to bishoprics and abbacies. For himself he undoubtedly desired the see of Canterbury, to which indeed he was formally elected on the death of William of Corbeil in 1136. For a translation, however, papal permission was traditionally a *sine qua non*, and Henry, in addition to his political foes, had powerful religious adversaries in the persons of St Bernard and other leading Cistercians. The abbot of Clairvaux in particular was a tireless agitator against one who by his political intrigues, his wealth, his martial exploits, his pluralism and his nepotism outraged, in the eyes of the reformers, not only the monastic but the Christian conscience of the whole of Europe, and the old wizard of Winchester or, still more forcibly, the whore of Winchester, figures in more than one of the saint's most lively letters.[1] Henry's election to Canterbury, therefore, was never confirmed. Consoled by a legation which set him above the new archbishop, Theobald, during several years he administered two dioceses

---

[1] Cf. the letters of St Bernard, ed. G. Hüffer, *Der heilige Bernhard von Clairvaux* (Münster, 1886), I 234: 'Philisteus tamen ille [*sc.* Henry of Winchester] in spiritu vehementi idolum Dagon [*sc.* William of York] juxta arcam Domini erigere non erubuit. Nonne ideo quia frons meretricis facta est ei? Divaricat crura, omni transeunti prostat et in questu pro meretrice sedet' (letter to Lucius II). Cf. *ibid.*, 234: 'Expectabamus ut vitis illa Wincestrie ... faceret uvas, sed conversa in amaritudinem vitis aliene fecit labruscas'. *Ibid.*, 236: 'Seductor ille vetus Wintoniensis'.

besides his own see and the abbey of Glastonbury; not content with this, he conceived the remarkable project of erecting Winchester into a metropolitan see with six suffragans. This scheme, too, foundered on curial intrigue or papal prudence, but Henry remained the most powerful ecclesiastic in the country till the death of Stephen, despite several maladroit political moves and sudden changes of front. Although he had favoured the young Henry and assisted him in his first days, the bishop of Winchester, an exceedingly overmighty subject with a group of private castles, was an anachronism in the new world of 1154, and having transferred the bulk of his funds abroad he followed them without asking for licence, and spent some years in reorganizing the finances and economics of Cluny, the monastic home of his few years in the cloister. He returned to England for good in time to consecrate, as *doyen* of the hierarchy, the new archbishop of Canterbury in 1162, and thenceforward was deeply concerned in all the phases of the controversy. Although Thomas had in the past been chiefly instrumental in obtaining the legateship for Theobald in opposition to the bishop of Winchester, and more recently as chancellor must have lent a hand in demolishing Henry's castles, the bishop bore no malice. Indeed, for all the adventures and intrigues and extravagances and ambitions of his middle life, which superficially seem to anticipate the worst characteristics of a Beaufort or a Wolsey, Henry had always remained not only blameless in his private life, but also unsoured, uncoarsened, unhardened and undefiled. All his contemporaries agree that in this last period of his life his character had greatly changed; perhaps it would be more true to say that the deepest potentialities of his personality, long undeveloped beneath the turmoil of ambitions and worldly activities, now had freedom to spring into life and view. Leaving intrigues and taunts to others, he became to all a venerable and beloved elder statesman, retiring further and further from his ambitions and even from his riches as he drew nearer to death. Consequently, his direct part in the great controversy was not large—one who had known him twenty years before could hardly have imagined him swept along so passively on the stream of events. Partly, no doubt, this was due to age, partly to a changed spiritual outlook, and partly to deliberate policy, but the deepest reason of all was perhaps a trait of character. Henry of Blois, though a very able, a curiously amiable, and in some respects even an admirable man, was not, either as a man of action or of thought, absolutely great. Though more resolute and more practical than his brother, he had something of Stephen's inconsequence. Neither his political nor his ecclesiastical activities were informed by far-sighted policies or ideals, or even by firm consistency; they were all intensely personal and opportunist. Consequently, in his last and most attractive phase the great issue made no challenge to him for a last and best fight. He passes through the pages of the *Materials* if not precisely as a ghost, a *revenant*, yet as something of a survival, as it might be a dowager with the light of a falling day about her. Nevertheless, Henry of Winchester was not in 1163 a volcano wholly extinct. His wealth, his influence, his venerable age, his legendary past, his amiable and devout present, all combined to make him a personality to be reckoned with.

(iii)

And now we come at last and as it were unwillingly to the most enigmatic figure of all, to the man of probity whom even a pope reverenced for his austerity of life, the mirror of religion and glory of the age, the luminary who shed a lustre even on the great name of Cluny;[1] the leader of the synagogue who raised the clamour for innocent blood; the Achitophel, who gave counsel as if one should consult God, against his master; the Judas, who made a pact upon the body of Christ, the church of Canterbury.[2]

Gilbert Foliot was a scion of a noble family of unknown origin which, though not counted in the invading armies, had yet come by the early decades of the twelfth century to own considerable estates in Oxfordshire, the Severn basin and Devonshire, and to be allied with the Earls of Hereford. In spite of the many literary memorials of his long and distinguished life the name of his father and the place of his birth are not known. His mother, as we have seen, must by inference from another relationship have been a Chesney, but the statement of a contemporary that he was a near blood-relation to Robert, Earl of Hereford, is not capable of verification from what is known of Milo's pedigree and marriage.[3] Gilbert himself tells us that he was a kinsman of Richard of Ilchester, later bishop of Winchester, who in his turn was probably a kinsman of Nigel of Ely and a member of the clan later known by the surname of Poor.

[1] *Materials*, V 42-4 (Alexander III to Gilbert Foliot in 1163); V 30-2 (Hugh, abbot of Cluny, to Foliot in 1163): 'Felix, inquam, Cluniacensis ecclesia, quae meruit talem habere filium, qui esset flos doctorum, religionis speculum, et praesentis saeculi decus'.

[2] For the parallels between Foliot and Achitophel, Doeg and Judas, *v.* John of Salisbury, *Materials*, VI 15. For Foliot as *archisynagogus*, the same to Bartholomew of Exeter, *ibid.*, VI 66. The comparison with Judas is hinted at by Archbishop Thomas, *ibid.*, V 516, and returned by Foliot, V 538.

[3] For Foliot's relationship to Milo, Earl of Hereford, and Roger his son, *v.* Florence of Worcester, II 91, Gervase of Canterbury, I 162 (*consanguineus* of Roger) and *Chronicon Angliae Petriburgense* (Caxton Society, 1845) *sub anno* 1130, where his brother Reginald is

The events of his life and that of his brother, a monk of Gloucester and later abbot of Evesham, suggest that his family connections with Gloucester abbey or one of its manors or dependencies were close. As a youth he was a student as a secular clerk, and was probably ordained priest, but there is no clear indication whether he studied at Paris or Bologna, or at one of the English centres such as Exeter; in any case it cannot have been for many years beyond his boyhood, though it was long enough to give promise, if not distinction, and he seems to have acquired the title of master, which had not yet to be earned by a course of specified length.[1] If a French school was the scene of his studies this would explain why, when he felt the call of religion, he should have sought Cluny, then ruled by Peter the Venerable, though indeed no personal reason is needed to account for the attraction of the greatest abbey of Europe, that still drew to itself a spiritual and social *élite*.

As has been remarked elsewhere, there was at Cluny in the early twelfth century a system, or at least a practice, by which the highest authorities hand-picked, if the expression may be allowed, promising young men, usually of good family, and placed them in key positions within the order, whence they rose, if they did not belie their promise, to the

nepos comitis Milonis Herefordiae. Milo's wife was Sibyl, daughter of Bernard de Neufmarché. For his relationship to Robert of Lincoln, *v. supra* p. 16 note 1, and Foliot's *epp.* 54, 221; as also *Gesta Abbatum S. Albani*, I 139, where he appears supporting the bishop, *cui sanguine jungebatur*, in the St Albans exemption suit. For Richard of Ilchester, *v.* Foliot, *ep.* 199.

[1] Hugh of Cluny, writing to Foliot in 1163 (*Materials*, V 30-1), refers to him as one in whom: 'scientia multarum artium vitiorum fuit interitus, non cumulus; qui mundanum philosophum vero Christo philosopho mutavit ... qui magistrum scholarum sic dimisit, ut discipulatum idiotarum Christi devotus addisceret'. I take 'magistrum ... dimisit' to mean 'abandoned his master'.

rule of one of the major Cluniac priories or allied abbeys, or were called by popes or kings to a still wider activity in an episcopal see or to become cardinals or papal legates. Gilbert Foliot was one of this class. He was already one of the priors at Cluny when he can have been little more than twenty-five, and he soon received promotion to the important priory of Abbeville.[1] It was in this capacity that he accompanied his great abbot, as he tells us himself, to the council of the Lateran in 1139,[2] and in the same year, through the direct action of King Stephen, who had heard of his high reputation, he was recalled to England to be abbot of Gloucester, whence his brother had recently departed to be abbot of Evesham.[3] Gloucester was a house of no more than moderate consequence, which had been raised to a high level of fervour and observance by its first Norman abbot, Serlo. Henceforward we can trace at least the external activities of Gilbert Foliot in his surviving correspondence—an extensive fragment, indeed, but not, considering his long years of administration and controversy, as inclusive as might have been hoped. This body of letters, which owing to its wealth of personal and local detail is of the greatest value for the church historian, stands badly in need of the critical editing which it is at present receiving. In its printed form it is treacherous for all save those who already have the events and personalities of the period clearly distinguished in their memory;

[1] Foliot to Henry II in 1173 (*Materials*, VII 556).

[2] Foliot, *ep.* 179 (to Brian fitzCount): 'Magno illi conventui, cum domino et patre nostro domino abbate Cluniacensi, interfui et ego Cluniacensium minimus'.

[3] Florence of Worcester, II 114-5 (*sub anno* 1139), attributes his appointment to Stephen: 'audita fama probitatis ejus eximiae'. This also implies connections with the west of England and the Severn valley (cf. John of Worcester, 54 *note*).

chronological order is lacking, an address is frequently lacking or given incorrectly, and misprints and false readings and erroneous extensions often conceal both names and ideas. Yet, for all its bulk, this correspondence tells us far less than we could wish of the character and outlook of the writer before the years of stress began. Very many of the letters are concerned with practical administration—with this or that canonical case or ecclesiastical difficulty—and though they are seldom purely formal, and are all written in Foliot's admirably clear style, they have none of Bernard's fire and charm, nor any of the literary interest and pointed wit of John of Salisbury. Foliot never writes of his own pursuits and feelings, nor are any of the letters preserved those of private friendship; still less does he permit himself *obiter dicta* on the doings and characters of others, though we know from an anecdote retailed by John of Salisbury, as well as from his own later outpourings, that he was not unaware of, or insensible to, the limitations of those in authority. We seem in his letters to be reading the day-to-day decisions of an ecclesiastical statesman—as it might be a Randall Davidson—rather than to the persuasions and the perplexities of a leader or a saint.

With these reserves, we can yet form a picture of the writer's character as it appeared for all to see. It is that of an able, efficient, prudent, tactful, eminently respectable churchman, a man in high position in a graded, orderly society, obeying and enforcing its laws with an equitable recognition of the tribes without the law—barons, it might be, and kings. He would seem to have taken particular pains to be on good terms with his colleagues; letters of recommendation and support are numerous, and when Roger of York took offence at something he had done Foliot was quick to write a dignified but complete apology

—he had shot his arrow o'er the house and hurt his brother.[1] We know from other sources that Foliot had the reputation of a man of letters and of an ascetic; he was a monk, and therefore had learned to obey and to be obeyed; the phrases of the Rule came readily to his mind and to his pen; and this prizing of external, formal obedience—'I also am a man subject to authority'—is not without importance as an ingredient in Foliot's character. He had been for many years a religious superior, and in outward behaviour and mental characteristics he bore the stamp of a dignified and cultured life—the life of the higher levels of the Cluniac family—to the end. Though he was in England throughout the troubles of Stephen's reign he never took to soldiering with Henry of Winchester, nor did he play for high stakes in politics. He remained throughout the abbot and the diocesan bishop.

During those years of anarchy he nowhere gives us his opinions on the great question of Church and State, papacy and empire or king, but it is clear from his actions and employments that he was a Gregorian of the Cluniac school: that is, he accepted the existence of a powerful, autonomous, privileged Church, obeying the canon law and the Pope; to him, however, all this was a matter of legal and diplomatic administration rather than a great reforming principle or a dynamic theological idea; in practice he was more of a Gelasian than a Gregorian. Foliot therefore, when the struggle came, had no past to rise against him. He was the just man who had no need for penance. Though

---

[1] Foliot, *ep.* 109. Foliot's own literary allusion is to an incident in the life of St Benedict (Gregory the Great, *Liber Dialogorum*, II vi): 'Ferrum de manubrio nobis inconsiderate moderantibus elapsum est'—a reminiscence of the episode of the Goth who lost his bill-hook in the lake at Subiaco.

there is a singular absence of the note of affection in all the many references to him by contemporaries, all agree that the correctness of his life and his unfailing regularity and ability command respect.

In the summer of 1148 he was urged by Archbishop Theobald to attend the council of Rheims against the king's command, and after some hesitation he went. Presumably he crossed the Channel by stealth in the small and ill-equipped fishing-smack, capable of carrying only a dozen men, in which Theobald made the passage.[1] It is tempting to suppose that among his companions on that uncomfortable and dangerous crossing was the archbishop's clerk, Thomas of London, who was certainly present at the council, but it is perhaps more probable that Thomas was one of those sent ahead to make the archbishop's official excuses for non-appearance. While Foliot was in France the learned and saintly Robert of Hereford, one of the three English bishops officially allowed to attend, died. Hereford at the time was controlled by the Empress, and Milo, Earl of Hereford, was Gilbert Foliot's near relation. At the proposal, therefore, of Theobald and with the approval of the Duke of Normandy his name was proposed to the Pope, who appointed him, apparently without any subsequent canonical election.[2] A difficulty arose as to his consecration, Hilary of Chichester and Jocelin of Salisbury, who were deputed by the Pope, refusing to function before

[1] John of Salisbury, *Historia Pontificalis*, ii, p. 8: 'Piscatoria navicula . . . que non plus quam xiii homines capiebat'.

[2] John of Salisbury, *Historia Pontificalis*, xix 47: 'Consilio et voluntate archiepiscopi Cantuariensis . . . placuit satis duci Normannorum.' John (p. 48) goes on to say that Gilbert hoped with Theobald's concurrence to hold the abbacy together with the bishopric, but the monks hastily elected a successor and had him blessed by the bishop of Worcester.

the king had given his approval. In consequence, Theobald himself performed the ceremony after administering to the elect an oath of fealty to the young Henry, which he took out of deference to majority opinion. This oath Foliot subsequently broke—a circumstance which should not be forgotten in the sequel.

When Theobald lay dying in 1160-1, and in the months of waiting that followed, Foliot, with all his experience and reputation to commend him, must have seemed to all disinterested observers the obvious choice of any electors. There was no other bishop and no other ecclesiastic, either of the career or in a monastery, who suggested himself. The canonical electors, the monks of Christ Church, Canterbury, would naturally have looked to him, though perhaps without excessive eagerness to have a Cluniac, for William of Norwich was an old man and they had no distinguished inmate of the cathedral priory to propose. The archbishop of Canterbury was *ex officio* in the place of abbot to the monks, and it was the current opinion, borne out by almost all the authentic information that was available, not only that the throne of Augustine should be occupied by none other than a monk, but also that it had almost always been so occupied. The rare exceptions of secular archbishops, such as Stigand, were not encouraging as precedents. It was therefore inevitable that Foliot should have regarded himself as a likely successor to Theobald, and it would have been only natural for a man of vigour and ability to desire the post. When abbot of Gloucester he had not refused (as had St Bernard) to become a bishop, nor in 1163 did he refuse (as did John Fisher later at Rochester) to be transferred to a more dignified see. That he did greatly desire election was the common opinion, shared by John of Salisbury and Archbishop Thomas, and the latter, at the most bitter moment of their contest, did not scruple to say so.[1] Foliot, indeed, both then and on another important occasion later, emphatically denied that he had canvassed for the position or used unlawful means of persuasion. This we may readily believe, but it is not a direct answer to the allegation that had been made, which was that he had been extremely desirous of election. His opponents went a stage further, and attributed to his desire for advancement his opposition to the chancellor's candidature. That he did oppose it strongly, that he was alone among the bishops and magnates to do so, and that he only desisted under a direct threat and command from the king seems certain from contemporary evidence.[2] This of itself is creditable rather than the reverse. No one could have foreseen the change that took place in the new archbishop, and for a worldly chancellor to be forced upon a recalcitrant electing body was a thing deplorable in itself and (so far as man could see) in its consequences. Indeed, we may feel that with such principles and in such a cause Foliot should have refused consent come what might: but we may feel also that when a great change had patently taken place in Thomas he should have ceased to cry scandal at the election of a worldly chancellor. It was not, however, in Foliot's

[1] John of Salisbury to Bartholomew of Exeter (*Materials*, VI 66): 'Qui quoniam, Deo aliter disponente, quod ambiebat esse non potuit Cantuariensis archiepiscopus, in Anglicana ecclesia . . . factus est archisynagogus'. Thomas to Foliot (*Materials*, V 517): 'Potuit autem fieri aliquas ecclesiasticas personas ad eandem promotionem, ut solet, adspirantes suspirasse'. Foliot denies it (*ibid.*, V 522-3, in 1166 and VII 556, in 1173), but he is primarily concerned to make it clear that he did not intrigue for the position.

[2] E.g., W. FitzStephen in *Materials*, III 36: 'Solus Gilbertus Herefordiae . . . quod potuit, dissuasit; ut putabatur non bene zelans electionem, sed male electum'.

character to say the last nay to the instant tyrant, or to allow a moral change in others to give entrance in his mind to a revaluation.

Whether or no he had desired or expected to go to Canterbury, Foliot, when once the prize had been given to another, must have been regarded with sympathy on every side. The most distinguished and exemplary churchman in England was now left, presumably for life, in the small, poor, and relatively unimportant see beyond the Severn. Almost at once Henry made a move by asking the Pope to allow Foliot to act as his confessor and mentor.[1] How far this was a purely religious move, or how far the loss of sympathy between the king and his new archbishop prompted Henry to take out a species of counter-insurance, must remain a matter of guesswork. A little later came the proposal to translate Foliot to the see of London, which had long been without an effective head, and which he had refused to administer in the king's interest while the former bishop was still alive. The proposal for translation was put by Henry to the Pope on the grounds that Foliot would be far more accessible as his adviser if he were in London. Archbishop Thomas wrote warmly to Foliot, urging him to accept.[2] There is no need to question the genuine goodwill of this letter. Personal spite and jealousy were never marks of Thomas's character, and even if he had not a more amiable motive he had won the greater prize and could afford to be generous, while on a lower level still it was in the highest sense politic to have Foliot as a friend

[1] Thomas to Gilbert in 1163 (*Materials*, V 29): 'Cum dominus papa tibi specialiter curam animae domini nostri regis commiserit'. Henry to Foliot (*ibid.*, V 24): 'Mihi ... cui saepius animae salubre consilium a cordis vestri procedens examine datum est'.

[2] Cf. letters of pope, king and archbishop in *Materials*, V 24-30.

rather than as an enemy. The harmony, however, was broken by an unexpected *démarche* on the part of Foliot. He refused to take the oath of canonical obedience to the archbishop. In the canonical wrangle which ensued in England and at the Curia his plea was that, having taken the oath to Canterbury once, it was unnecessary to repeat it on translation. The canonical issue, indeed, proved to be a nice point, and Alexander III fluctuated in his answers; at one moment he certainly wrote to Foliot allowing him to omit the oath.[1] Contemporaries, on the other hand, saw in the incident a proud *non serviam* to the ex-chancellor. The true reason for his refusal is almost certainly to be found in an intention, conceived from his first acceptance of the bishopric of London, though abandoned when more pressing controversies broke out, to vindicate the metropolitical status of the see. This claim of London to be a third archbishopric, based on a phrase of a letter of Gregory the Great, which may have reflected a tradition of pre-Saxon English Christianity, had been put forward by Richard Belmeis I under Anselm.[2] Nor did Foliot lack other precedents. Twenty years previously Henry of Winchester had tried to put through a scheme for his see which had far less historical foothold; and at almost the same time the canons of St David's, in an endeavour to

---

[1] *Materials*, V 55-6; 60; 130; VI 591; IV 224-5. It seems clear that in 1169-70 Foliot, whose original contention had been that a profession once made need not be renewed, because still valid, used his successful refusal as evidence of his independence of the archbishop. Cf. *Materials*, VII 40-3 and W. FitzStephen, *ibid.*, III 88.

[2] For the original arrangements of Gregory the Great *v.* his *Epistolae* XI 65, and Bede, *Historia Ecclesiastica* (ed. Plummer), I 63-4. For a revival of the pretensions of London under Bishop Richard Belmeis I, *v.* Anselm's *epp.* III 152. For a further discussion of Foliot's claim, *v.* Appendix III.

establish the freedom of their bishop from Canterbury, had appealed to ancient authority for an arrangement in the distant past when London had been the seat of an archbishopric and Canterbury had not.[1] Foliot, with his long experience and his Hereford connections, must have known of all this and resolved to exploit his knowledge. It should in justice to him be observed that although in a move of his at Northampton, and again at a crisis in 1169, he appeared to regard himself as free of obligations, at other moments in the years that followed his election he did in fact by his words and actions admit that he owed obedience to the see of Canterbury. His original refusal was, however, an unfortunate move, for it inevitably embroiled the good relations so recently and precariously established between Thomas and his rival.

In the pages that follow we shall have many occasions for noting the actions of the bishop of London. It is unfortunate that we possess no life of him by a friendly contemporary, and not even so much as a character sketch. He would seem to have been a reserved man, with few intimate friends, and to have inspired respect and even admiration, but little affection. Chroniclers and writers who praise Bartholomew of Exeter and Roger of Worcester, and who speak with warmth, and even with affection, of the elderly Henry of

---

[1] Mr C. N. L. Brooke has suggested to me the three stems of this tradition: (1) The legendary foundation of the three archdioceses of London, York and Caerleon *temp*. King Lucius (Geoffrey of Monmouth Book IV, ch. xix); (2) the legend often resuscitated by the claimants on behalf of St David's metropolitical status, that there had been five provinces in Britain (*v*. J. Conway Davies, *Welsh Episcopal Acts*, introd., pp. 190-232); and (3) tradition influencing Gregory the Great (Cf. Arles conciliar list in Haddan & Stubbs, *Councils*, I 5, with bishops of London and York, and *E.H.R.* LII 354 *note*) in favour of London.

Winchester, make no comment on Foliot. Had he died in 1162 he would be remembered as an eminently able and ascetic prelate of unblemished reputation, *omnium consensu capax imperii*. It is his share in the great controversy, and his recorded actions, and still more his letters, that disquieten us. Gilbert Foliot, unlike Archbishop Thomas, did not change. His icy current and compulsive course kept due on. Disappointed ambition, perhaps all the more painful because unacknowledged, the unwillingness to admit virtue in the recently converted publican, an inborn dislike of anything noisy or violent, of any trace of *panache;* the strong personal bias; the unfortunate series of accidents which made him an almost *ex officio* leader of the opposition and advocate of the king—all these contributed to make of Gilbert Foliot the adversary of his archbishop and, once adversary, his talents and reputation made him inevitably the one to whom all who opposed the archbishop looked for leadership and counsel.

(iv)

We have now passed in rapid review the provenance and careers of the bishops. It would be to travel far beyond our theme to consider the causes and events of the controversy between the king and his archbishop, but it is perhaps necessary to look, however rapidly, at the ecclesiastical world of Europe—what we may almost call the ecclesiastical climate of Europe—during the twenty-five years preceding Clarendon, when the majority of the bishops were in office or at least in active life as churchmen. A neglect of this larger canvas, and an almost exclusive attention to domestic and administrative detail, has given to many of the older accounts of the struggle a narrow, if not wholly false, perspective.

The middle decades of the twelfth century were part of an epoch in which both ideas and men circulated with the greatest freedom throughout western Europe. Concentration on English topics—feudalism, administration, manorial organization—should not be allowed to lead to oblivion of this. On the Continent three great spiritual and intellectual streams were flowing strongly and widely in the early part of the century and, like the Severn tide, were often running at their height far up among the meadows when in the open sea beyond the bar the waters were hanging ready to ebb. There was, first, the wave of the Gregorian theory of church government, implying universal papal surveillance and cognizance; secondly, there was the even stronger and wider wave of theological and legal progress; and, finally, there was the still more universal flow of religious zeal manifesting itself in the new foundations of canons and monks and knights—Cistercians, Premonstratensians, Gilbertines, Templars and the rest. All these were at full flood in the 1140s, and would under any circumstances have poured, or at least seeped, into England. Actually, as has been so clearly shown in recent studies, the weakness and the predicaments of Stephen left the door into this country wide open and, theoretically at least, the Church in England was for twenty years untrammelled. As Z. N. Brooke wrote: 'Freedom had now come to mean both freedom from lay control and freedom to obey the laws of the Church, especially the new reforming decrees, freedom, in fact, to be as the rest of the Church was'.[1] Moreover, during these years the study of theology and of canon and civil law was ever growing in depth, and was presenting to all the most eager and able minds the concept of a highly organized and centralized Church, administering a uniform

[1] Z. N. Brooke, *The English Church and the Papacy*, 176-7.

system of jurisprudence, while the idea of the Roman Curia as a universal court of appeal, to which any case could at any moment be transferred, gained ground everywhere. Each year these ideas were affecting more and more young men of English and Norman blood at Paris, Bologna and the other schools. Their education done, these men joined the *familia* of a bishop and often passed in the course of their career from a household of the second rank to one of the first, till at last they themselves became prelates; others among them might take up residence at the Curia and thence rise to a cardinal's dignity, or be sent back to their native country as bishops. When they had become Ordinaries, they might often find themselves employed as papal judges-delegate to administer the canon law and report to the Pope or ask for his guidance. All these influences, powerful as they would have been in any region —for, like the ideas of the sixteenth-century Reformation or of the French Revolution, they were dynamic and accorded well with the spirit of the age—these ideas were irresistible in the days of Stephen and breached at every point the ring-fence which William the Conqueror, living in a world of other ideas, had thrown round his *landeskirche*.

In consequence, the bishops whom we have been examining were almost all, in greater or lesser degree, men of Europe and familiar with the papacy in action. Hilary of Chichester had been a curial advocate; he was appointed by the Pope and consecrated at his order. Bartholomew of Exeter was a Parisian theologian and a canonical expert. Gilbert Foliot had been present at the councils of 1139 and 1148; he had been appointed by the Pope. All these three bishops were frequently employed as papal judges-delegate, as was also Roger of Worcester. William of Norwich had been at the council of 1148 and was another favourite choice as judge-delegate and assessor to the archbishop. Jocelin of Salisbury was the personal friend of Alexander III and had had frequent official relations with the Curia. Of Henry of Winchester enough has already been said to show his position. Robert of Hereford was a celebrated Paris theologian and Roger of Worcester had been his pupil. Roger of York had often journeyed to the Curia on behalf of Theobald, and later in his own interest. Nigel of Ely had visited Rome more than once, and had had frequent relations, both sweet and bitter, with the papacy; Robert of Lincoln must certainly have visited Rome, even though the circumstances of his interview with the Pope may be mythical. Several of the bishops, as we have seen, had, so to say, invested in the papacy by obtaining bulls of protection and confirmation for their cathedrals and households, even before 1160, and many of them were active patrons of the new international orders. The list of such connections with Europe and with Rome could be extended indefinitely.

This then was the climate of opinion in which Henry II had to work. His aims and actions were consistent throughout his reign, save when they were thwarted by the living and posthumous influence of his first archbishop of Canterbury.

CHAPTER III

THE COUNCILS OF WESTMINSTER, CLARENDON AND NORTHAMPTON

(i)

THE controversy in which the colleagues of Archbishop Thomas played a great and in some ways a decisive part reached its first crisis in the series of meetings and discussions which opened at Westminster in October, 1163, and closed at Northampton almost exactly a year later. On the course and issue of these discussions we possess a mass of information copious even to embarrassment. Although on the highest intellectual levels the age of the humanists was giving place to that of the scholastics, the men who were thirty or forty years of age in 1163 had all had a wide literary education, and were both able and eager to record and to comment upon the great events at which they had been present and the great personalities whom they had known. Thirty years earlier, Abelard had told the history of his calamities, and twenty years later a monk in private place in an East Anglian abbey felt impelled to set down, for whose eye we know not, a picture of a great abbot and his monastic society that has become classic. It need not surprise us, therefore, to find that the contemporaries of Thomas of Canterbury and Gilbert Foliot were well aware of the significance and of the dramatic interest of the happenings of their time. In fact, there are nearly a dozen detailed accounts of the events of 1163-70, and though the inter-relation of several of these has set historians many complicated problems, there are at least seven highly individual narratives, two or possibly three of which were written by those who had taken part in, or had at least been silent witnesses of, the events they describe.[1] We have what purport to be the very words used by the principal actors, and often their speeches at considerable length, and though we are naturally and justly critical in their regard, it is well to remember that among the younger men who surrounded the king and the archbishop were some of the most brilliant, agile and receptive minds in western Europe. Intelligences were as clear, and memories as retentive, then as now. The

[1] Any discussion or review of the biographical material for Archbishop Thomas would be out of place here. In general, the evidence as to dates and relationships put forward by M. E. Walberg, *La tradition hagiographique de saint Thomas Becket avant la fin du xie siècle* (Paris, 1929), seems to me plausible, and his arguments have governed the selection of passages for reference. The complicated questions of interdependence are in practice less important than they may at first appear: thus, e.g., even if the somewhat surprising conclusions be accepted that John of Salisbury, when writing his short *Life*, made liberal use of William of Canterbury, and that the well-informed *Life* of I Anonymous ('Roger of Pontigny') follows closely the metrical French *Life* by Guernes, the fact remains that both John and the anonymous writer knew the archbishop well, and had copious first- and second-hand knowledge of the events they narrate, and hence could have adopted from others only that which they knew themselves to be true or highly probable. In reconstructing the story it is manifestly impracticable to give in all cases reasons for adopting this or that version; preference has usually been given to William FitzStephen and Herbert of Bosham, who were both at the archbishop's side in England during 1162-4 and 1170 (December), while Herbert was also his inseparable companion abroad. The narratives referred to in the text are William of Canterbury, John of Salisbury, Alan of Tewkesbury, William FitzStephen, Herbert of Bosham, Edward Grim, Benedict of Peterborough, Guernes and the two anonymous printed in *Materials* as I and II. To these must be added the anonymous Icelandic saga, based on a lost *Life* by Robert of Cricklade.

council of Northampton, as the conference of Versailles, had its Maynard Keynes and its Harold Nicolson.

All accounts agree that during the first fifteen months of Archbishop Thomas's episcopate relations between him and the king were steadily deteriorating. At the deepest level this was due to the widening rift in the aims of the two men, resulting in the shock of warring characters, the wounded pride of the king turning from affection to bitterness, the archbishop losing all but his deepest affection and loyalty in disillusion at what to him seemed the self-will and duplicity of Henry. But between two such powerful characters, set at the head of Church and State, the opposition could not remain on the level of private emotion; both men in the years 1162-3 were going their own divergent ways—the king gathering into his hands all the threads of government and control, the archbishop reclaiming or asserting a claim for the Church in respect of all the possessions and rights which in his eyes had been lost within the recent past. Among these rights was that of the omnicompetence of the ecclesiastical tribunals in so-called spiritual cases, and in particular the right to judge and pronounce sentence on clerks charged with criminal offences. This, as has been well observed, was an issue on which a firm and final settlement could never be found, at least in a society which acknowledged a unique and strongly centralized religious authority, but it was an issue susceptible of compromise when moderation and goodwill existed in both parties. These qualities were lacking in England in 1163, but the matter of criminous clerks was not in truth the issue over which the great contest was fought. That issue was the broader and more essential one of the overall control of the Church by the secular authority, expressed ultimately in the demand of the king for the adhesion of all churchmen to the customs, reputed ancestral, of the kingdom and of the royal government.

At what precise moment and through whose agency the question of the customs emerged as the crucial issue is not altogether clear. According to John of Salisbury, who was still in England at the time, and who was undoubtedly a most acute observer, the first suggestion came from those in the king's service who had received or who feared injury from the vigorous action of the archbishop.[1] The first occasion on which the ancestral customs came forward as a living issue was, it would seem, the council which opened at Westminster on 1 October, 1163. Some of our informants, indeed, assert that the explicit purpose of the king in summoning this council was to get adhesion to the customs, but these writers use the vaguest language, while the few who attempt greater precision agree that the council was summoned, ostensibly at least, for other business, and that the customs came to be considered on a sudden motion. An anonymous brief account of these years has it that the sole agendum of importance was the examination of the claims of Canterbury to be the primatial see of all England, as against Roger of York, and that suddenly and unexpectedly an attack was made on the archbishop.[2] It is possible that the charge made against Roger of being cause of all the evils may rest on some such basis as this. From another, and wholly independent,

---

[1] John of Salisbury (*Materials*, II 309), referring to events before October, 1163: 'Multos et magnos elegit [diabolus] discordiae incentores, per quos', &c.

[2] *Summa causae inter regem et Thomam* (*Materials*, IV 201): 'Sola autem et summa causa concilii [*sc.* of 1st Oct., 1163] fuit haec, ut metropolitanus Cantuariensis totius Angliae primas esse solemniter monstraretur'.

source we learn that at Westminster was decided the great exemption suit of St Albans, and that no less a person than Ailred, abbot of Rievaulx, was among the assembled prelates.[1] John of Salisbury says nothing of all this, but asserts that the council had been summoned for routine business and that it so happened that a controversy arose between Church and State.[2]

For the sequence of events at Westminster Herbert of Bosham, who asserts that he was present, may be followed as probably giving us the truest account. According to him the question of criminous clerks was the cause of the meeting;[3] the matter was debated, and some at least of the bishops were disposed to yield; the archbishop of Canterbury, however, together with the archbishop of York, was constant in opposition, and eventually the whole body of bishops were firm in supporting him.[4] It was with a view to shifting the ground of his attack on their position that the king, who had just appealed to a charter of Henry I, enquired if they were prepared to keep the ancient customs of the realm. A discussion among the bishops followed, after which they replied that they assented to the customs in so far as their position as ecclesiastics allowed (*salvo*

---

[1] *Registrum Antiquissimum of Lincoln* (ed, C. W. Foster, Linc. Record Soc., 1931), vol. i, no. 104, pp. 64-6. From another source (*Chronicon Angliae Petriburgense, sub anno* 1163) we learn that Ailred was present, and preached, at the Translation of Edward the Confessor a few days later (13th Oct.).

[2] John of Salisbury (*Materials*, II 310): 'Convenientibus autem episcopis et proceribus, ex mandato regis, ad expediendas regni necessitates, orta forte contentio est inter regem et ecclesiam, &c'.

[3] Bosham (*Materials*, III 266, 273-4).

[4] So Guernes, ed. Walberg, line 849, and he is as a rule no friend to Roger.

ordine suo).[1] This reply was given by all singly, including Roger of York, save for Hilary of Chichester, who to placate the king substituted the words *bona fide* for the saving clause of the rest. His action, however, pleased nobody. The king spoke roughly to him and demanded from all an unconditional assent, and when the assembly broke up, exhausted and with nothing settled, the archbishop turned on Hilary and rated him for using a different form of words without having consulted his colleagues. On the following day the king, having reclaimed from the archbishop the castles of which he still had custody from the days of his chancellorship, departed before daylight, unknown to the bishops; several of these, alarmed, followed him in their anxiety to get on good terms, and the archbishop soon found himself with few supporters among his colleagues. With them he waited for some change in the king's attitude.[2]

It is at this point, probably, that we must put the intervention of Bishop Arnulf of Lisieux. That prelate of doubtful reputation has recently found an apologist,[3] but it is difficult to acquit him of double-dealing. On the present occasion, so we are told by several of the archbishop's biographers, Arnulf had come to England to win his way back into the good graces of the king. Arriving in the thick of the trouble, he is said to have exploited the occasion by telling Henry that his policy should be to drive a wedge

[1] Bosham (*Materials*, III 273): 'Ad quod archipraesul, praehabito tamen cum fratribus suis consilio, illas respondit se et fratres suos observaturos, salvo ordine suo'.

[2] Bosham, *ibid.*, 274-5. W. FitzStephen omits all account of the Westminster council.

[3] G. Barlow, in *The Letters of Arnulf of Lisieux* (Camden Soc., 3 ser. LXI, 1939), introduction.

into the hitherto solid phalanx of the bishops.[1] Arnulf had no doubt already sounded Roger of York and Hilary; in any case they, and Gilbert Foliot, were the obvious nucleus of an opposition to the archbishop, and for them Henry is said to have sent. They were amenable to persuasion, and Hilary forthwith sought out Archbishop Thomas at Tenham. His arguments were twofold: that the king had in fact power to act as he pleased with or without the bishops' consent; and that he also in fact had promised that no uncanonical action would be required as a consequence of the bishops' promise. The former argument was not one to impress Thomas; to the latter he replied that while the king could keep the bishops to their part of the undertaking, neither they nor anyone else would be able to keep him to his.

Hilary of Chichester was not the only visitor who came to the archbishop. During the two years from the autumn of 1162 to that of 1164 Alexander III was at Sens, and therefore unusually accessible to English envoys. During the last months of 1163, indeed, Arnulf of Lisieux is said to have crossed the sea six times on his way from and to the Pope. Henry was still *persona grata* with the Curia, and was now complaining that the archbishop by his importunate claims and intransigent behaviour was dislocating English church government and imperilling good relations between the king and his clergy. The Pope, therefore, and some of the cardinals wrote to Thomas urging moderation, and the letters were brought by no less a person than the abbot of L'Aumône, the abbey that had been the favourite daughter of Clairvaux.[2] Philip, abbot of L'Aumone, had for long been St Bernard's prior, and had left Clairvaux for

[1] Will. Cant. (*Materials*, I 14); Grim, *ibid.*, II 377.
[2] Guernes, line 866.

his new charge soon after the saint's death. He was an advocate of unusual moral power, and he was accompanied by the archbishop's old master of Paris days, soon to be bishop of Hereford, Robert of Melun.[1] Thomas was assured by the abbot that the king wanted no more than a formal assurance to satisfy his *amour propre* and keep him in countenance with his lay barons. Hitherto, it must be remembered, no precise terms had been suggested for the ancestral customs. Overcome, the archbishop yielded, and in the last weeks of the year he proceeded to Woodstock and offered to accept the customs in all good faith, thus using the very phrase for which he had a few weeks before taken Hilary of Chichester to task.[2] If he had hoped that this would make a complete reconciliation possible, he was soon undeceived. Henry's affection for his ex-chancellor had perished for ever; he seized eagerly on the submission and declared that it must be as public as the previous opposition had been. ·

(ii)

The meeting for this purpose took place at the royal palace of Clarendon near Salisbury on 14th January, 1164. As soon as the king had formulated his proposals the archbishop saw clearly (what no doubt he had already feared) that the abbot of L'Aumône had unwittingly deceived him and that something much more than a formal token of respect was required. It is unfortunate that the two biographers who were probably present—William FitzStephen and Herbert of Bosham—say little about Clarendon, but there is no reason to doubt the circumstantial and on the whole consistent account of several other sources. According to these, the archbishop for long maintained silence,

[1] So Guernes, 881 (I Anon. in *Materials*, IV 31).
[2] Guernes, 910 (I Anon., IV 32).

thus tacitly breaking his engagement with the king to give his colleagues a lead. These, confined in a single room, debated the situation for more than two days.[1] Though many of them had previously yielded in private to the king's demands, they had probably, like the archbishop, hoped that by so doing they had escaped all further molestation. The demand for a public recantation of their solemn assertion of rights at Westminster was too much for them. The vehement and precise language of Gilbert Foliot, writing two years later to the exiled archbishop, can scarcely be altogether false. According to him, all present stood firm with their leader even when, on the third day, their deliberations were interrupted by an inroad of barons vociferating threats and going through a pantomine of violence.[2] Foliot, however, is guilty at least of suppression of the truth. Not only does he tacitly omit Roger of York from his list of stalwarts, but we look in vain for the name of William of Norwich. Now the archbishop's biographers tell us that a principal reason for his yielding was compassion for the plight of two of his colleagues, the bishops of Salisbury and Norwich, with whom the king had already old scores to settle. This was, however, not the only motive with Thomas. The king was in a fury—this is one of the occasions to which the biographers apply a favourite text: 'as the roaring of a lion, so is the anger of a king'—and threats of personal violence had been clearly directed not only against the bishops of Salisbury and Norwich but against the archbishop himself. Nevertheless, he had stood firm against the appeals of his two colleagues, and against

[1] Foliot to Archbishop Thomas (*Materials*, V 527): 'Inclusi eramus omnes conclavi uno; die vero tertio', &c.

[2] *Ibid.*, 527: 'Regni principes ... conclave quo sedebamus ingressi, rejectis palliis exsertisque brachiis', &c.

the warnings of the Earls of Cornwall and Leicester, who had informed him of the danger in which he stood and begged him to prevent the fearful scandal which would ensue if the king mutilated or executed a batch of bishops. Finally, the archbishop was approached by two eminent Templars who repeated with variations the arguments of the abbot of L'Aumône, maintaining that the king was only jealous of his dignity and rights, and that he would never abuse the powers granted him. They expressed themselves willing to stake their eternal salvation on this.[1] This argument, impossible to disprove and perhaps invidious to question, could only be resisted by one whose clarity of vision was equalled by his detachment from human ties. In a later century another ex-chancellor was at the moment of

[1] Bosham (*Materials*, III 279) says: 'Haec tamen ut induceretur potissimum causa fuit, caritas videlicet fraterna et compatiens'. W. FitzStephen, *ibid.*, III 48, differs; he says: 'timore mortis, et ut regem mitigaret'. Will Cant., *ibid.*, I 17, and the usually well-informed Guernes (lines 938 *et seqq.*) say that it was the cumulative effect of the appeals of the two bishops, two earls and two Templars. There is a curious disagreement, however, as to the bishops concerned. The biographers who mention names (Will. Cant., *ibid.*, I 16, Guernes, 938-9 and Grim, II 381) give Jocelin of Salisbury and William of Norwich. The I Anon (*ibid.*, IV 34), who had Guernes before him, strangely gives Jocelin and *Roger* of Norwich, and continues with a description of Roger of Worcester. Bosham (*ibid.*, III 279), who was present, but who wrote twenty years later, gives Jocelin and Henry of Winchester. It seems certain that Salisbury and Norwich were the bishops concerned. No source tells precisely why these two were obnoxious to Henry, though there is frequent reference to Jocelin as *persona non grata*. For a partial probable explanation, *v.* note 2, p. 21 *supra*, and the support Jocelin had given to the archbishop's clerical policy (*Materials*, III 264). The connection of William of Norwich with a refusal to pay scutage rests on a doubtful interpretation of a phrase in a letter of Theobald to him, suggested by A. Jessop in *Dict. Nat. Biog.*

trial steadfast in the face of a very similar appeal.[1] Thomas of Canterbury was not yet so well prepared, and he was overcome.

We do not know with absolute certainty what form his acquiescence took. Some authorities imply that it was frank and full; Foliot, who says that the resolve was taken on a sudden while the archbishop was apart from the rest, tells us that he exclaimed bitterly that he was being forced to take an oath which he could not keep and for which he would soon be doing penance. Another source suggests that he and others applied the flattering unction of casuistry; by swearing to observe the customs truly and in good faith they could *ex hypothesi* be understood only to bind themselves to such of the practices as were canonical, since an uncanonical practice was *per se* a bad one, and a bad one could never become technically a *consuetudo* but remained an *abusus*. A similar argument in a later century was equally futile. Whatever the mental reservation employed, the archbishop, with an appeal to the king's mercy, made the promise. Henry seized upon his words. 'You have heard the archbishop's free assent; it remains for the bishops to follow him at his command'. Thomas gave the order and all took the oath.[2] Only Jocelin of Salisbury, strangely enough, remained motionless, and when the rest had

---

[1] *The Correspondence of Sir Thomas More*, ed. Rogers, p. 521, where More says to Margaret Roper, after an allusion to Bishop Fisher: 'Verely, Daughter, I neuer entend . . . to pynne my soul at a nother man's backe, not euen the best man that I know this day liuing; for I knowe not whither he may happe to cary it'.

[2] One biographer certainly, two possibly, may have been present, and we have also Foliot's account. W. FitzStephen (*Materials*, III 48) asserts that the archbishop stood out long against his colleagues ('annitientibus episcopis diu restitit, diu contradixit') and then acquiesced ('adquievit ad tempus assensu et in verbo veritatis

promised, asked the archbishop what he should do. He was bidden to take the oath with the rest, and had a reprimand from Henry for his pains.

With the assent of the bishops behind him Henry now demanded that the laws and customs of the past should be set down in writing, so as to avoid any future misunderstandings.[1] Once again the archbishop saw how worthless had been the arguments that had been used to win him. When the writing, to be celebrated as the constitutions of Clarendon, was presented, it comprehended a whole programme, and he was asked to put his seal to it. This apparently he did not do, alleging the need for further deliberation on such an important matter, but he accepted one of the three copies of the chirograph of the constitutions.[2] On the first day at Clarendon he had been in good

stipulatione'). Bosham (*ibid.*, III 278-9) says: 'in omnium conspectu et primus ante omnes archipraesul in praetacta forma se obligat . . . quasi juratoriam adjiciens cautionem, hoc se facturum in verbo veritatis confirmavit'. Foliot (*ibid.*, V 527-8) makes out that the bishops were unanimous in resistance, but that the archbishop after private deliberation suddenly declared his resolve to perjure himself by making the promise. That Thomas was the first to give the undertaking, and was then required to command the others to do so, seems certain.

[1] The clear statement of Bosham (*Materials*, III 279) that this had not been done previously seems conclusive.

[2] W. FitzStephen (*Materials*, III 48) says definitely that he sealed them ('sigillorum suorum impressione'). But Bosham, who was certainly present, says as explicitly that the archbishop did not sign, but temporized (*ibid.*, III 288: 'non de plano negat, ad differendum dicebat adhuc'), and that he was then given one part of the chirograph. John of Salisbury, II 312, Grim, II 383, Will. Cant., I 23, Guernes, 1010, and I Anon., IV 37, agree with Bosham's account, and this is doubtless the correct one; it is borne out by the archbishop's statement to John of Poitiers cited by the latter, V 112: 'Deo enim incessanter gratias refero, quod (sicut ex aliorum

spirits; now he was depressed. On the road home he was told that Hilary, first author of the substitution of the words *bona fide* for *salvo ordine nostro*, was coming to join them. 'Let Satan stay behind me', he remarked.[1]

Successful in obtaining the assent of the bishops to the constitutions of Clarendon, Henry proceeded a step further. Relying on his services to the Pope, then in exile at Sens, he wrote himself, and required the archbishop to write also, asking for papal approval to the constitutions. From what happened afterwards it would seem that an exact copy was not sent, and that the archbishop was able to convey a sense of disapproval—which was indeed made clear enough by the penance which he was doing for his fault, and by his request for absolution.[2] The Pope's reply came in a little over a month—perhaps early in March—refusing approval to the constitutions and exhorting the archbishop to be firm.[3] Meanwhile, the king had asked also of the Pope for

fida relatione, et nunc tandem ex rescripti vestri fide, certissime teneo) detestabiles illas ... consuetudines ... non absolute ... observandas promisistis, neque, ut ceteri, scripti vestri munimento roborastis'.

[1] Bosham (*Materials*, III 292). Henceforward the *Materials* will be quoted by volume and page only.

[2] Grim, II 383; Guernes, 1036.

[3] V 84 (Alexander III to Thomas, ? Jan., 1164); 85 (the same to the same, 27th Feb., 1164); 88 (the same to the same, 1st April, 1164). English historians have not always made it clear that it was Henry, not the archbishop, who first brought the constitutions to the Pope's notice, and that the papal condemnation arrived several months before the meeting at Northampton. It is not therefore correct to represent Thomas as forcing the Pope's hand. The letter from Alexander to Thomas, printed in *Materials*, V 53, and dated by the editor 26th October, 1163, should probably be dated 1164; it replies to a letter probably despatched from Northampton immediately after the council.

a legation over all England for Roger of York. This, if granted, like the similar one obtained by Henry of Winchester twenty-five years before, would have effectively deprived the archbishop of Canterbury of all leadership and initiative. Alexander, having supported Thomas on the major issue, followed the normal course of Roman diplomacy by granting what he could to the loser, and gave the desired legation; it was, however, so limited as to be innocuous, and Henry after a time returned the instrument in disgust. Meanwhile the archbishop, now at least clear in mind and conscience, was in fact disregarding the constitutions and sounding his colleagues with a view to resistance; here, however, he had little success, and feeling that events were moving towards an impasse, he twice attempted to cross the Channel to visit the Pope. This was a direct contravention of the constitutions and confirmed Henry in his course of active hostility. From the various pleas and quarrels already in existence he selected the case of John the Marshal, whose appeal from the archbishop's court to the king's had been disallowed by Thomas, and accused the archbishop, who had failed to obey the royal summons, of contempt of the royal jurisdiction.

(iii)

The assembly at Northampton, which was convoked for 6th October, 1164, differed in many respects from the council at Clarendon. At the latter the archbishops and bishops, forming a body of considerable solidarity, had been as a group the object of attack on an issue of high ecclesiastical policy—the conduct of the courts and relations with Rome. At Northampton the issue was ostensibly one of royal justice only. The bishops were present simply as normal members of the great Council, and, since the archbishop's double *volte-face* at Clarendon and after, they had become a group without a leader rather than a body with a head. At the same time, many of them must have been uneasy at their submission and secretly in approval of their archbishop's latest position, though not, perhaps, of his impulsive and, it may have seemed, secretive conduct.

Few gatherings in medieval history are more rich in moral and dramatic interest or have been recorded in greater wealth of detail than the council of Northampton. We have at least seven long narratives and a number of shorter accounts, and of the seven two at least are the work of men who were present at the archbishop's side through-out.[1] As is to be expected, there are numerous disagreements and discrepancies in detail, some of which are not susceptible of resolution, and while on the whole we must follow the two eye-witnesses, William FitzStephen and Herbert of Bosham, who, especially when they agree, have every claim on our belief, yet several of the others add numerous facts, from whatever sources they may come, which explain or support the two principal narratives.

On the first day on which the assembly got down to business, Thursday, 8th October, there was a long discussion, at the end of which the archbishop was judged to be guilty of contempt of the royal jurisdiction in having neglected to obey the royal summons to court, and to have forfeited all his movable goods to the king's mercy. When, however, it came to pronouncing sentence a difficulty arose,

---

[1] The seven principal narratives are those of Herbert of Bosham, William FitzStephen, William of Canterbury, Alan of Tewkesbury, Edward Grim, Guernes of Pont S. Maxence, and the I Anonymous. The two first were the archbishop's clerks. For the chronology of the council, *v.* Appendix IV.

neither the barons nor the bishops wishing to shoulder the responsibility. The barons complained that they were mere laymen, while the bishops retorted that this was a secular, not an ecclesiastical, court, and that they, the bishops, could not be asked to condemn their superior. Finally the king insisted that all should take part, and laid the obligation of pronouncing sentence on the bishop of Winchester. The archbishop at first refused to acknowledge the court, but in the end submitted. He was judged to have forfeited all his movable goods to the king, and all the bishops became his guarantors, with the significant exception of the bishop of London.[1]

The day had undoubtedly been one of success for the king. The archbishop had been encountered on a terrain where his canonical foothold was slippery; he had at first taken a high line and then yielded. Similarly the bishops, bound by feudal loyalty and the Clarendon oath, had at first writhed and then given way, thus losing the advantage of a gracious compliance with the king, while becoming awkwardly embroiled with their chief. The guarantee which they gave on the archbishop's behalf was an attempt to satisfy another loyalty, but here, too, neither king nor archbishop would give them any thanks. Henry would probably have been well advised, had peace been his genuine desire, to rest upon his success and dismiss all thoughts of further charges against the archbishop. That, however, it was not in the king's character to do.

The logical sequel to the condemnation of the archbishop for contempt of the king's summons to his court would have been the trial before Henry of the case of John the Marshal, whose appeal from the archbishop's jurisdiction

[1] So William FitzStephen, III 53.

had provided the king with a useful weapon.[1] Here, however, Henry was on weak ground. The archbishop's judgment had probably been just, the Marshal had avoided perjury only by a subterfuge, and the sympathy of all the great lords of honors was with the holder of a baronial court. Henry therefore dropped the case, and was for reviving the issue of criminous clerks, but his advisers pointed out that this would reunite the bishops and their metropolitan, so the king proceeded to a series of demands that were frankly punitive. The first of these was for money received from the castelleries of Eye and Berkhampstead. No previous notice had been given of this and the money had been spent in the royal service, but the archbishop, still hoping for peace, accepted the obligation, for which three lay barons stood guarantors. The king's next demand was for large sums borrowed by the chancellor for the siege of Toulouse and other purposes; the king claimed that these were a pure loan and pressed for judgment. Once more the bishops were forced to condemn their leader, and once

---

[1] The course of events in the case of John the Marshal, like other incidents of the controversy, has often been treated confusedly. John had claimed land at Mundham, in the manor of Pagenham, in the archbishop's honorial court. Disappointed in his suit, he made use of the recent constitution by which appeal could be made to the king's court from any lord's court for reasonable cause. John's oath that justice had been denied him was, so the archbishop claimed, made on a service-book (a troper) not on the gospels, which, besides being an offence in itself, was fair proof that he was attempting to escape the technical guilt of perjury. The king then summoned the archbishop to present himself at court on the feast of the Exaltation of the Cross (Sept. 15th). FitzStephen and Foliot assert that the archbishop refused to attend, and the former asserts explicitly that no claim of sickness was made (cf. W. FitzStephen, III 52; 'citatus a rege neque venerat, neque corporis infirmitatem ... allegaverat'; and Foliot, in his letter of 1166, V 530: 'Non est a vobis

more laymen, five in number, stood as guarantors. But it was not money, nor even a forensic triumph, that Henry wanted; he wanted to break the archbishop, and he now demanded accounts for all receipts from vacant bishoprics, including Canterbury, and abbeys held by the chancellor during his term of office. This was of course a wholly outrageous demand. The moneys had in fact been the equivalent of revenue, received and spent by a royal official, and the absence of any adverse comment either at the time or later would in itself have been in equity equivalent to a discharge, even if this had not been, as Thomas alleged, formally given. Moreover, the archbishop was now legally penniless, with all his friends deeply engaged on his behalf. Further obligations could only have meant

[sc. Thoma] haec admissa citatio, verum vos in hoc sibi minime pariturum declaravit a vobis ad ipsum [sc. regem] delegata responsio'). On the other hand, William of Canterbury and Grim (and their derivatives) say that the archbishop was sick and sent excuses and full legal arguments; cf. Will. Cant., I 30: 'quia die responsionis graviter aegrotasset'; Grim, II 390: 'cum adesse non posset gravi detentus infirmitate.' H. Bosham's words (III 296) are ambiguous. The contradiction thus would seem to be absolute, without the possibility of harmonization. It may be noted: (1) that if the archbishop had in fact been ill and alleged this plea at Northampton, it is hardly conceivable that all his colleagues would have condemned him for contempt of court; (2) that the earliest witness, Foliot, writing to the archbishop himself, makes no mention of this plea; against this must be set the many inaccurate statements of Foliot's letter; and (3) that the similarity between the first alleged illness and the second (at Northampton) is exact, even to the king's disbelief in its authenticity. The source of all references to the earlier illness may well be William of Canterbury, who was not a monk, and perhaps only a child, at the time; he may well have made one incident into two. On the whole, therefore, it seems probable that illness was not alleged by Thomas in the case of John the Marshal.

imprisonment or the dismemberment of the archbishopric. Thomas demanded time for counsel with his colleagues, and the meeting broke up on the Friday evening. The following days were occupied with ceaseless negotiations, and it is not surprising that the accounts present numerous difficulties. Fortunately, the two eye-witnesses, Fitz-Stephen and Herbert of Bosham, give the fullest accounts, and with numerous indications of time and day. They are not always in perfect agreement; Herbert wrote many years after the events, and we can follow FitzStephen with more assurance.

The demand for accounts had been made on Friday, 9th October. On the morning of Saturday all the prelates came to the archbishop's lodging at St Andrew's, and he consulted both bishops and abbots separately. Of the abbots' counsel nothing is known, but the speeches of the bishops have been reported in some detail. Although the accounts are at variance, it must have been at this first meeting that the archbishop repeated that he had been given full quittance on the king's behalf on the day of his consecration. Henry of Winchester, the consecrator, now he came to think about it, remembered the incident clearly;[1] it was in fact common knowledge, and the bishops in a body waited upon the king to remind him of this. Henry, however, refused to be put off, whereupon the bishop of Winchester, to whom money was no object, tried an offer on his own of 2,000 marks.[2] But it was not cash that the

[1] H. Bosham, III 300: 'Henricus tunc Wintoniensis episcopus . . . tandem recordatus est', &c. It is a curious phrase; but Bosham was writing many years after the event.

[2] W. FitzStephen, III 54: 'concilio nobilis Henrici Wintoniae episcopi . . . qui ei ad hoc auxilium validum promisit . . . et obtulit ei duo milia marcarum'.

king wanted—indeed, as the event showed, he was no longer working to a rational plan at all. Once more the bishops took counsel with their head. It is at this point that one of the biographers, who was not himself present or even in England at the time, but who nevertheless had access to good sources, inserts a short summary of the advice given to Thomas by his colleagues.[1]

Gilbert Foliot, as dean of the province, began by reminding the archbishop of his lowly origin, of the royal benefactions to him, and of the ruin to which he was bringing the Church in England. He therefore advised resignation. Henry of Winchester, the father of the bench, took a different view. The archbishop's resignation, he thought, would set a most pernicious example. In the future, any prelate who had a difference with the king would have to resign. Canon law, not personal or political considerations, must be the decisive criterion. Hilary of Chichester followed. The advice of the bishop of Winchester, he said, was excellent for ordinary times, but in the present predicament everything was at sixes and sevens, and a prudent economizing was more likely to win through than a rigid adherence to the canons. He therefore advised a discreet submission, which would be better than a forced retreat from an extreme position. After him came Robert of Lincoln, characterized as a simple and indiscreet man. To him the matter was plain. The king, he said, was seeking the archbishop's life, and what good would the arch-

---

[1] Cf. Alan of Tewkesbury, II 327. Alan was probably out of England at the time, and for some years a canon of Benevento, but as Canon Robertson noted (II, introd., xliv), he may well have had details from the archbishop of Benevento, Lombardus, who had been an intimate companion of the archbishop in exile (H. Bosham, III 524).

bishopric be to a dead man? Bartholomew of Exeter followed: the days were evil, he said, and only by a compromise could the storm be weathered. The present attack of the king was personal and not general; the archbishop must be sacrificed rather than the whole Church. Finally Roger, the elect of Worcester, was asked his opinion, but refused to give it explicitly. To counsel the archbishop's resignation would be against his conscience, he said; to advise resistance to the king would be to put himself at the bar with his metropolitan. Whatever the historical accuracy of these declarations, the general impression of indecision and lack of firm support for the archbishop may be taken as a fair reflection of the prevailing frame of mind. Archbishop Thomas, we are told, decided to temporize, and sent the bishops of London and Rochester to the king with the message that those who knew most about the accounts were not yet at Northampton, but that on the next day of the council he would answer as God might show him. Foliot, according to one account,[1] did his best to commit the archbishop by conveying the message in a different form: the archbishop, he announced, requested a brief delay in order to present his accounts. When, however, the Earls of Leicester and Cornwall came to say that the king would agree if that was indeed the reason for delay, the archbishop disclaimed all responsibility for the message in that form. He would come, he said, God helping, and would answer as it should be given him.

The first meeting of the bishops mentioned above probably took place on Saturday. All Sunday was likewise spent in unofficial discussions, and it may have been on that day that the opinions recorded by FitzStephen were expressed. He was present throughout, and is undoubtedly

[1] Alan of Tewkesbury, II 329.

the most trustworthy witness. According to him some of the clerks urged the archbishop to stand firm; he had committed no crime and need fear no judgment. Others urged resignation, and Hilary of Chichester is reported as having wished that the archbishop could become plain Thomas again.[1] He reminded the archbishop that he, the ex-chancellor, knew the king better than any of them; he knew then that resistance was useless; if he did not yield the king would act.

Discordant as these witnesses may be on details, it is clear that until the Sunday evening there had been a great deal of enervating and indecisive discussion and nothing more. Though individuals among the bishops wished Thomas well, and were even willing to give him sturdy counsel, the hierarchy as a group had lost solidarity, and would neither give encouragement nor promise support to their chief. They were, indeed, still shackled by their oath at Clarendon. Yet in their defence it may be said that hitherto the archbishop had given them no clear lead—he had, indeed, twice without warning turned suddenly in his tracks—and had made no direct appeal to ecclesiastical principle. The initiative, in fact, still lay with the king.

On Sunday night the archbishop was taken ill.[2] The illness, a complaint to which he was from time to time subject, was, whether organic or not, doubtless brought on, as the biographers remark, by the prolonged psychological and emotional strain of the past few days, by his apprehensions for the future, and by the uncertainty of mind that preceded his great decision. Until the Friday it would seem that he had never utterly abandoned hope of

[1] W. FitzStephen, III 55. 'Utinam posses esse non archiepiscopus et remanere Thomas.'

[2] For the archbishop's illness v. Appendix V.

some solution that would leave him as archbishop in England, in some kind of tolerable relationship with the king. Now all that was clearly out of the question. To resign the archbishopric would be to deny that his actions had been guided by any principle, and would, in addition, leave him in private place entirely at the king's mercy. To fight the king on the formal, legal rights of the case would probably be vain, and in any case would put him in a false position bereft of his spiritual authority. He had moreover received reports, which grew in weight on Monday, that the king intended to have him, when condemned, executed, mutilated or imprisoned out of hand.[1] How far the two more violent courses were real possibilities we cannot know. Henry II was not by nature bloodthirsty or utterly ruthless, nor had the machinery of government attained the cold relentlessness of the Tudor age. Still, it is clear that the archbishop himself, and some at least of his informants, considered the physical danger real; it is fairly certain that, had all gone as the king wished, imprisonment would have been his fate, and there was nothing Thomas dreaded more than the inactivity of a long confinement which would deprive him of all possibility of speaking and acting in the name of the Church in England. In this strait he sought advice from his confessor, prior Robert of Merton.[2] Whether or no the biographers have preserved this man's speech correctly, his recorded words certainly embody the

[1] Will. Cant., I 32: 'Sermo percrebuit, et a nobilibus quibusdam Thomae nuntiatum est, quod si sui copiam faciet in curia, vel trucidaretur vel in carcere teneretur'. For an elaboration on the same theme, *v.* FitzStephen, III 65.

[2] Prior Robert's part is told most fully by I Anon., IV 45, and Guernes, 1547. He was Robert II, prior of Merton 1150-67, succeeding Robert I, who had been master of the young Thomas (FitzStephen, III 62); cf. *Victoria County History of Surrey*, II 102.

principles of the archbishop's subsequent action. 'Act fear-lessly', he said. 'Had you so wished, and had you regarded worldly success alone, you could long ago have been at perfect peace with the king. You chose instead God's service; the issue therefore is God's concern; He is all-powerful and cannot fail'. And he bade him say next morning a votive Mass of St Stephen, who had not feared to give testimony before a council.

The scenes of the following day, Tuesday, 13th October, are among the most celebrated in English domestic history. The archbishop, against all expectation, had recovered; he was visited in the early morning by agitated bishops who had heard that trial and condemnation as a traitor were awaiting him; the general advice was that he should resign and submit himself unreservedly to the king. The archbishop replied with bitter force: 'The sons of my own mother have fought against me'.[1] During the past days, he added, the bishops, instead of supporting him, had twice given judg-ment against him in a civil case; now he feared that they would do the same on a criminal count. This he forbade them to do under pain of suspension, and appealed to Rome against them.[2] Moreover, he commanded them to excommunicate forthwith any who should lay violent hands upon him. As for himself, he would stand firm. While the others heard this in silence, Gilbert Foliot im-mediately lodged a counter-appeal against the archbishop's

[1] Bosham, III 303. Cf. Canticle of Canticles I, 5 (Vulgate): 'Filii matris meae pugnaverunt contra me'.

[2] III 305. This first appeal is omitted by most biographers; Bosham's statement is, however, corroborated by FitzStephen, III 62, who also, when telling of the later appeal on the Tuesday, makes Thomas say (64): 'Unde et eos [sc. episcopos] appellavi . . . et adhuc appello'. The point of Foliot's first appeal was that the archbishop was forcing him to break faith with the king.

last command; the bishops then left St Andrew's for the castle, save for two, who remained for a few minutes to express their sympathy for the archbishop and to hearten him. The two were Henry of Winchester and Jocelin of Salisbury.

The archbishop then celebrated Mass with its significant Introit *Etenim sederunt principes* and its still more significant gospel with its reference to Zachary slain between the temple and the altar.[1] Then, still wearing some of the priestly vestments under a cloak, preceded by his cross, and carrying secretly the sacred Host to serve as Viaticum should the worst befall, he took horse for the castle.[2] Then took place a famous incident. Dismounting in the courtyard, as the gate shut behind him, he took from his bearer the archiepiscopal cross. Some bishops were at the door of the castle, among them Gilbert of London. One of the archbishop's clerks, Hugh of Nunant, later bishop of Coventry, approached him: 'My Lord of London, can you stand by while the archbishop carries his own cross?'. 'My dear fellow', replied Foliot, 'the man always was a fool and he'll be one till he dies'. Robert of Hereford, his old master,

---

[1] The Introit is from Ps. 118 (P.B.V. 119, 23): 'Princes also did sit and speak against me; but thy servant is occupied in thy statutes'. The gospel is from St Matthew, xxiii, 34-9.

[2] Bosham, III 303-5. Thomas had wished to go to the king in his Mass vestments, carrying his cross, but was dissuaded by the two Templars (Bosham, 304), presumably Richard of Hastings and Tostes of St Omer (Walberg, pp. 236-7, notes on Guernes, lines 958-9). Bosham (305) notes that he carried the Host: 'Secum ipsemet sed clam ecclesiasticae communionis portabat viaticum, eucharistiam scilicet'. His cross was a solid piece of work, for the four knights, six years later, had thoughts of braining him with the haft (I Anon., IV 71). For a note on the plan of the castle of Northampton. *v.* Appendix VI.

tried to take the cross from him in vain; Foliot, approaching on the other side, told the archbishop sharply that he was a fool, and he also endeavoured to wrest the cross from him. Roger of Worcester rebuked Foliot: 'Would you prevent your Lord from carrying his cross?', only to be told sharply that he would live to be sorry for those words.[1] The bishops then fell aside and Thomas entered alone, bearing his cross, and passed through the hall himself; the others followed, and Foliot again remonstrated: 'Let one of your clerks carry it'. Thomas refused. 'Then let me have it; I am your dean; do you not realize that you are threatening the king? If you take your cross and the king draws his sword how can we ever make peace between you?' 'The cross is the sign of peace', answered Thomas. 'I carry it to protect myself and the English Church'.

The wrangle over, the bishops drew away from the archbishop, who had now entered the inner chamber, and he sat alone, with two clerks, who were to be his biographers, at his feet, waiting for the worst that could happen.[2] At this tense moment a touch of bitter comedy, not unobserved by one of the clerks, was provided by the

[1] All the biographers have this incident, though they differ in detail; it seems clear that both Robert of Hereford and Gilbert Foliot tried to wrest the cross from the archbishop, the former from respect, the latter in anger. There can be no certainty that Foliot's well known taunt was spoken directly to Thomas. FitzStephen (III 57) says explicitly that (as in the text) Foliot was replying to Hugh of Nunant, but the bishop of London may well have felt that the words would bear repetition.

[2] I Anon., 47. 'Rex enim et archiepiscopus seorsum et non in uno loco constituti erant.' H. Bosham, III 307, tells us that the king was upstairs and the archbishop in an inner room (not the hall) on the ground floor. He himself was sitting at Thomas's feet, with Fitz-Stephen (cf. III 58), but everyone else drew away: 'archipraesulem vero alloquebatur nullus'.

entrance of Roger of York. He had arrived late to the council, partly to ensure attention, like a queen at the theatre, partly, so the chronicler suggests, to have a secure alibi should he be charged with having worked the archbishop's downfall. He now entered, with his unpermitted cross borne before him, and there were thus two crosses in the castle, as it were two hostile lances at rest.[1] The bishops were then summoned to council with the king, who had retreated to the upper floor at the news of Thomas's advent.

Arrived upstairs, the bishops found that Henry had been taking counsel how to proceed. He had at first intended to charge the archbishop with the cases of criminous clerks over which there had been controversy, but it had been pointed out that this would unite the bishops in common cause with their chief. Now he had heard of Thomas's appeal against the bishops to the Pope; this was one more direct breach of the undertaking given at Clarendon. He therefore sent a deputation to the archbishop to ask him whether he was prepared to exhibit the accounts of his chancellorship and give sureties for his debts; it was also asked whether he stood by his appeal. Thomas answered at some length: as for the moneys spent as chancellor, he had received formal quittance; as for guarantors, his colleagues and friends were already too deeply engaged to undertake more; as for the appeal, it had been lodged against suffragans who had condemned him against justice and ecclesiastical precedent; he therefore held to his prohibition and appeal, and commended himself and the

[1] W. FitzStephen, III 58: 'ut conspectior ingrederetur et de consilio illo regis non videretur; qui et suam e regione anticrucem sibi praeferri faciebat, quasi "pila minantia pilis"' (Lucan, *Pharsalia*, I 7).

Church of Canterbury to the Pope. The barons who formed
the party of enquiry received this reply with mixed feelings;
some were silent and sympathetic; others angry or bitter;
and a few recalled within earshot of Thomas some interesting precedents, such as Odo of Bayeux, Stigand and Arnulf
of Séez, with barbaric details.[1]

Henry, cognizant of the archbishop's reply, called the
bishops, and required them to join with the barons in
judging and sentencing the archbishop. They were in an
awkward predicament.[2] Though the court and case were
ostensibly purely feudal, they were both by training and
conviction committed to the canonical authority of archbishop and pope; confused as they were, they were not
prepared, either at this crisis or later, to cut the cord which
bound them at one and the same time to Canterbury and
Rome, and they knew that in any appeal to Rome their
locus standi would be greatly weakened by an overt act of
disobedience. The king insisted: the oath they had taken
at Clarendon, he said, destroyed the validity of the archbishop's prohibition. Nevertheless the bishops still held
out; some would not, others dared not, pronounce a
criminal sentence on the archbishop.

It seemed that a deadlock had been reached. Passions
were rising, both among the barons, who were exasperated
by the delays and frustrations, and among the bishops, who
were divided in counsel and sympathies; a small group
were bitterly remorseless, while the others refused to act.

---

[1] Grim, II 394; I Anon., IV 47; W. FitzStephen, III 63-5:
'Stigandum Cantuariensem archiepiscopum nigranti injectum puteo,
perpetuo carceri damnavit. Pater etiam domini nostri regis . . .
Arnulfum Sagiensem electum et plures clericorum ejus fecit evirari'
(with barbarous additions).

[2] H. Bosham, III 308: 'res enim in arcto erat', &c.

Down below in the inner room sat Thomas, while between him and the bishops and the king there passed a ceaseless interchange of question and reply.[1] In the general desperation Henry of Winchester came down to beg him to resign; since there was a real danger of a wholesale attack upon the bishops. Thomas refused; he had not taken office to resign it, he said, but to spend himself for it.[2] Then Roger of York appeared, calling with some ostentation to his clerks to come away with him so as not to witness the terrible fate of the archbishop.[3] This, we are told, unnerved Bartholomew of Exeter, who fell on his knees before the archbishop, begging him to yield, while Jocelin of Salisbury and William of Norwich, against whom old scores still stood, joined in the appeal. The archbishop sat on, as if cut from Marpessian marble. Finally, those most friendly to Thomas used every endeavour to find a way out of the impasse. They gathered the three arch-enemies, Roger of York, Gilbert of London and Hilary of Chichester, and represented the danger to themselves and to the realm if violence were done, in their presence and with their consent, to an archbishop for whom their hatred was notorious; they then took counsel together to find some way of getting rid of him while keeping their own hands clean. They decided at last to promise the king that, if he would excuse them from pronouncing judgment of the archbishop, they would forthwith lodge an appeal to the Pope, and would accuse Thomas of perjuring himself and forcing them to disobey

[1] I Anon., 47: 'mediatoresque verbi inter eos [sc. regem et archiepiscopum] erant episcopi, qui frequenter huc illucque discurrebant'; W. Cant., I 35: 'intermeantibus aulicis qui regis ad ipsum et vicissim verba referrent'.

[2] Grim, II 395.

[3] For Roger of York calling his clerks, v. Alan of Tewkesbury, II 331.

against their oath; they would further undertake, when in the Pope's presence, to obtain the archbishop's deposition.[1] This proposal, which was not only made but immediately adopted, appears at first sight an extraordinary one under the circumstances, and none of the biographers gives any hint of its significance or origin. Seen without a background, it seems a strange concession to demand of the king, while in view of the Pope's expressed opinion of the king's claims it is not easy to see how such an appeal could have been expected to be successful. The course proposed, however, was not a haphazard expedient devised by Foliot or another. It has not, I think, been noted that it was precisely the procedure recommended by Gerhoh of Reichersberg in his treatise *De Novitatibus hujus temporis*, which we are told was presented to the English Pope Adrian IV at Benevento in the winter of 1155-6.[2] In it Gerhoh discusses the propriety of the Church holding the *regalia*, that is, the large estates bestowed by the king at appointment, together with the obligations and duties which their possession entailed. He is on the whole content that the bishops should hold these *regalia* and accept the obligations incurred, and that they should be expected to take the oath of fidelity to the king *salvo sui ordinis*

[1] For the agreement to appeal cf. I Anon., 49; W. Cant., I 37; H. Bosham, III 308-9. The latter (p. 322) tells us that those went to Rome who had bound themselves to the king to appeal.

[2] Gerhoh of Reichersberg, an Augustinian canon (*M.G.H.*, Libelli de Lite, III 132) was a reformer with moderate Gregorian views. His *Liber de Novitatibus hujus temporis* (edited by E. Sackur in *Monumenta Germaniae Historica*, Libelli de Lite, III 288-304) was presented to the English Pope Adrian IV at Benevento between 21st Nov., 1155, and 10th July, 1156. A. J. Carlyle, *Medieval Political Theory in the West*, IV 342-83, has a good general account of his doctrine.

officio. What, however, was to happen if the bishop violated this oath? Was the Church, i.e. the bishopric, to be deprived of all its possessions, while the bishop continued to hold office? And was the king to take matters into his own hands as judge and entrust his knights with the execution of his decisions? No, answered Gerhoh, the matter is to be referred to the bishop's superior (the word is vague, and Gerhoh is apparently thinking of the metropolitan rather than the Pope), who, if he find the prelate guilty, is to deprive him of office, after which the king in his own court can deprive him of the *regalia*, thus leaving the field completely clear for a new election. It would, Gerhoh adds, be a preposterous situation if the king were to do all the judging and the *regalia* and estates were to be plundered by his knights.[1]

---

[1] *Liber de Novitatibus*, ed. Sackur, 297. 'Ergo sicut illi [*sc*. Abraham and Abimelech] sibi mutuo juraverunt, sic adhuc reges jurant justitiam ecclesiae cum consecrantur et coronantur, et episcopi quoque regalia tenentes regibus jurant fidelitatem salvo sui ordinis officio. Si ergo fuerit violatum jurisjurandi sacramentum, violator, licet sit abbas aut episcopus, jure utroque spoliatur honore [*i.e.*, civil and ecclesiastical] coram suo judice, sacerdotali scilicet et illo quem de regalibus habet. Si enim perjurus episcopus tenens episcopatum, spoliandus regalibus exponatur militibus, inde consequetur confusio magna, qua invalescente minuentur et vastabuntur ecclesiastica bona dum nimis incaute abstrahentur ipsa regalia, et ita scindetur pallium Samuelis, quo scisso scindetur et regnum et periclitabitur sacerdotium'. Cf. *ibid.*, 297-8. 'Episcopi qui primo regulariter electi et spiritaliter examinati atque consecrati postremo propter imminentem necessitatem super albam vestem [*i.e.* the bishop's office] suscipiunt et purpuream [*i.e.*, the secular position] ne hac repudiata periclitetur ecclesia ipsis commissa. Qua si obrepente perfidia in regnum commissa judicabuntur spoliandi, veste simul alba sunt privandi, ne item periclitetur ecclesia cum sui honoris integritate illi auferenda et alteri committenda, ut sola puniatur persona perfida, ecclesia permanente in integritate sua, quoniam, ut dictum est, quae Deus conjunxit non est bonum ut homo separet'.

How far this suggestion was original to Gerhoh and whether it was in fact acted upon in Germany is not clear, but the remedy proposed, as will be seen, is precisely that brought forward by the bishops to the king, with the substitution of the Pope for the indeterminate 'superior' of Gerhoh. The plan, in fact, if carried through would have appeared an extremely shrewd one, for it held out to the archbishop's enemies the possibility of complete canonical disgrace, while his friends may well have realised that the Pope would refuse to play his part. In any case, it saved the bishops for the moment from both the king's anger and a canonical *faux pas*. We are not told precisely, and cannot guess, who was the proposer of the scheme. Herbert of Bosham says that it issued from the common deliberation of the bishops, but as he also tells us that those who had promised to implement it were chosen for the embassy to Sens it is natural to suppose that either Roger of York or Gilbert of London was responsible, and there is some evidence, as we shall see, that Foliot was in other respects influenced by the ideas of Gerhoh.

As for Henry, he had no intention of waiting for the papal decision and meanwhile he had the bishops committed to a united attack on Thomas before the Pope. He therefore agreed, and the whole group once more approached the archbishop, still seated in the lower chamber. Robert of Lincoln, we are told, was in tears, others were near weeping, and this must surely have been one of the several occasions on which, so we are told, his emotions got the better of Ralph of Diceto.[1] Hilary of Chichester, as always, found the words. The bishops, he said, had good reason to com-

---

[1] W. FitzStephen, III 65. 'Flebat Robertus Lincolniensis et quidam alii lacrymas vix continebant'. *Ibid.*, 59. 'Similiter et Radulfus de Dicito . . . plurimum ea die ibi lacrymatus est'.

plain of their head; they were already in a tight enough corner, and his prohibition had put them fairly between the hammer and the anvil.[1] First of all he had bidden them make a promise at Clarendon, and now he had prohibited them from honouring that promise. For this reason, and to guard against further harm to themselves, they had agreed to obey his latest prohibition and to appeal to the Pope against him. Despite his perilous situation, which this did little to mend, the archbishop felt a sense of relief.[2] The bishops had obeyed his prohibition, and there was nothing he would welcome more than a chance of meeting them in trial before the Pope. He therefore replied that at Clarendon he had given his word with the proviso that nothing uncanonical should be asked of him, but that in any case the Pope had subsequently condemned the constitutions. Two wrongs did not make a right; no one was bound to keep an oath which he should never have taken. If all fell at Clarendon, all could rise now. With this answer the bishops returned to the king and were excused from taking part in the trial; then returning, they sat with the archbishop below.

The climax of the long day was now at hand. The archbishop was seated, holding his cross. With him sat his suffragans, who, as a body, had appealed to the Pope against him. In an upper room, near enough for the angry cries of 'Traitor'! to be heard by those below, were gathered the barons, stiffened by the addition of the sheriffs

---

[1] W. FitzStephen, III 65. 'In angiportu magno nos inclusistis, quasi inter malleum et incudem nos misistis.'

[2] Grim, II 396: 'archiepiscopus laetus quidem appellationem amplectitur'.

and lesser men.[1] In such a gathering the issue was certain, and the archbishop was condemned and sentenced—to what, never appeared, but probably to that perpetual imprisonment which he most dreaded. While the king and a few others remained, the main body of the council came down the stairs to pronounce sentence.[2] The archbishop did not rise to meet them, but remained seated, still holding the cross. Proceedings did not begin at once, as none of the leaders of the council was anxious to act as spokesman; some still had sympathy with the archbishop; still more had Regan's dread of a spiritual father's malediction.[3] These men, it must be remembered, were not the fawning time-servers, the Riches and Audleys, who surrounded Henry VIII, but the founders of abbeys and the friends of saints.

Finally, after the duty had been passed round, the Earl of Leicester, a man of good report with all the biographers, took up the unwelcome tale. He began with a long recital of the archbishop's debt of gratitude to the king, and passed on to a minute account of the events at Clarendon. It was clear that he feared to come to the point. The archbishop saw his opportunity; breaking in on the earl, he forbade anyone present to pass judgment on him. Leicester was shaken, but began again, still more slowly, then exclaimed that he would not do it, and bade the Earl of Cornwall take his place. He too boggled, whereupon Hilary of Chichester, to expedite matters, said that the treason was clear, and

---

[1] H. Bosham, III 307: 'Omnes igitur passim et manifeste proditorem conclamabant ... Et super hoc clamor invalescebat unde et audientes haec per totam aulam tremore et horrore concutiebantur'.

[2] Grim, II 397-8; H. Bosham, III 307.

[3] W. FitzStephen, III 67; H. Bosham, III 309; I Anon., IV 50-1.

bade the archbishop hear the judgment.[1] Thomas rose, exclaiming that it was none of their business to judge their archbishop, and strode through the hall towards the door. There was an uproar, some calling him traitor, others gesticulating and hurling rushes and other débris into the air.[2] In the press, the archbishop stumbled over a cord of faggots by the central hearth and there was more shouting and jeering. Hamelin, the king's illegitimate half-brother, again shouted 'Traitor!'; Thomas, turning on him, gave him the lie as a lout and a bastard. 'If I were not a priest', he exclaimed, 'my hands should prove my honour on you'.[3] And thus, in the biographer's phrase, they departed from the council. The gate of the bailey was locked, but the porter was scuffling with a private enemy, a bunch of keys hung on the wall unguarded, and a clerk found the right one. Thomas rode across the town acclaimed by the people.

There was no pursuit. According to one biographer Roger of York and Foliot immediately advised the king to take no violent step in the crowded and excited town, but to send for the archbishop at some future date and imprison him; according to another, it was Robert of Hereford who

---

[1] W. FitzStephen, III 67. 'Comes Legecestriae ... coepit negotium Clarendonae habitum articulatim commemorare ... at ... Hylarius Cicestrensis episcopus, quasi inde manifesta erat regiae majestatis laesio ... dicebat archiepiscopo, quod suum audiret judicium. Sed non plura passus, ait archiepiscopus', &c.

[2] Grim, II 398: 'impetu facto contorta stramina et levia quaeque quae occurrebant jacientibus'.

[3] W. Cant., I 39. 'Hamelinum ... vicissim improperans ... garcionem et spurium.' I Anon., IV 52. ' "Si liceret", inquit, "et miles essem, propria manu te mentitum probarem".'' The incident is mentioned without Hamelin's name by Herbert of Bosham (III 310). Grim's statement (II 399): 'Vir Dei nemini quicquam respondens', cannot be accepted though he is followed by Guernes, 1930: 'Li sainz huem ne dist mot, mais avant s'en ala'.

represented to the king that any violence would prejudice his cause.[1] Actually, perhaps, the attack on the archbishop, like a cavalry charge, had got out of hand and overswept its objective, and Thomas's unexpected move had non-plussed his opponents. In any case Henry made proclamation that the archbishop was not to be molested, though we need not take too seriously Foliot's later account of Henry as another David, begging his knights to save him the boy Absalom.

The events of the day, grave and pregnant with consequence though they had been, had not altogether broken relations between Thomas and his colleagues. While he was at supper the bishops of London and Chichester called upon him, to announce that they had found a way to peace. When the archbishop asked the formula, they suggested the temporary transference of two Canterbury manors. The archbishop replied that the king already held one of them unjustly, and that he would never give away the property of his Church.[2] After supper he sent for Walter of Rochester, Robert of Hereford and Roger of Worcester, the three bound most closely to him, and asked them to wait upon the king with the request for a safe-conduct to the coast. They found Henry in good spirits; he replied that he would give an answer next day.[3] At midnight, as we know, in pitch darkness, wind and torrential rain, the archbishop, disguised and with only three companions, left

[1] W. FitzStephen, III 69 (Robert of Hereford); W. Cant., I 37 (Roger of York and Gilbert of London).

[2] Alan of Tewkesbury, II 334.

[3] W. FitzStephen, III 69. There is divergence among the biographers here; FitzStephen says permission was asked to depart simply; Grim (II 334) says to go to Canterbury, Bosham (III 312) to go abroad.

the town through an unguarded gate. With the fortunes of his Odyssey we are not concerned.

Early next morning Henry of Winchester arrived at St Andrew's to call on the archbishop; he asked his chamberlain what he was doing. 'He is doing very well', was the reply; 'he has departed, no one knows whither'. 'God's blessing go with him', the bishop, so we are told, replied. The other Henry's comment was different: after a moment's wrathful silence, 'We have not done with the fellow yet', he observed.[1]

When the archbishop's flight became known the council met again; though the whereabouts of the fugitive were uncertain it was assumed that he was bound for Sens. The king therefore had to present his case; meanwhile, the canonists among the bishops were sufficiently influential to persuade him to leave the possessions of the archbishop intact, as by canon law they should be, pending the appeal.

We may now look back for a moment on the series of meetings between the autumns of 1163 and 1164. It cannot be said that Archbishop Thomas had showed either statesmanship or steady devotion to principle. Having originally taken up a rigid and extreme and perhaps unpractical attitude in defence of ecclesiastical immunities, he had with some difficulty persuaded his colleagues to stand with him, thus securing a unity which would have made the bishops invincible, especially with the added moral support of the Pope, which would have been forthcoming. Nevertheless, suddenly and without taking counsel, he had abandoned this position and had commanded his colleagues to follow

[1] I Anon., IV 54-5. 'Cui occurrens Osbernus, beati viti camerarius ... interrogatus ab eo quidnam ageret archiepiscopus, "Bene", inquit, "agit", &c. ... Rex autem ... "Nondum", ait, "finivimus cum isto".'

him in pledging themselves to action in a contrary sense. Then, just as suddenly and without counsel, he had abandoned and condemned his new course of action. This time, however, there was no immediate occasion for him to rally his colleagues.

When next the summons came from the king, the bishops were no longer acting as spiritual counsellors, but as vassals of a feudal monarch, and the archbishop was no longer their leader but in the position at first of a defendant and later of an accused. The king as feudal monarch had a strong case against the archbishop, who on the most favourable showing had treated his summons in a very cavalier fashion, and who had shown his irresolution both by attempting, and by failing, to leave the country without licence against the promise of Clarendon. Had Henry been moderate, he could have discredited and financially embarrassed the archbishop at the expense of a very little injustice. He chose instead to satisfy his hatred, and thus not only turned the sympathies of many once more towards the archbishop, but by pressing the criminal charge in a matter of treason he reduced to an absurdity the contention that the bishops were present simply as feudal barons. To admit this would have been to admit in principle that in any issue of ecclesiastical privilege the accused might be judged by his colleagues as a vassal. No doubt it was a confused feeling of this that disposed the bishops to receive in so docile a fashion the archbishop's prohibition to sit in judgment on him. It was then that Thomas, by another sudden wrench of policy, regained the initiative which he had lost nine months previously and stood out once more as a champion of liberty. But by his flight, secret and sudden as his earlier moves had been, he left his colleagues without a leader and without a policy.

CHAPTER IV

THE CONDUCT OF THE BISHOPS, 1164-70

THE sequence of events during the six years between Christmas, 1164, and the return of the archbishop to England in November, 1170, is extremely difficult for the historian to set out and for the reader to follow. The biographers of the archbishop and still more the chroniclers are, as is only to be expected, very arbitrary in their choice of the events to be recorded; all of them, even the faithful and long-winded Herbert of Bosham, omit without notice months and even years. Meanwhile, side by side with the narrative sources runs the great collection of letters, priceless indeed as a sure foundation and authentic commentary on the events, but capricious in the light it throws, now extremely full on a small issue, now lamentably defective on a great one, and abounding throughout in dropped threads and roads that lead nowhither. To these difficulties we may add the lack of precise dating and the order and ascription of the documents as printed—sometimes demonstrably wrong and often very probably so. Something of this desperate disorder has crept into even the fullest modern accounts; they are, almost without exception, incomplete and confusing.

No attempt can here be made to give a full narrative; we are concerned solely with the parts played by the bishops. But while it will be simplest to take each of the leading prelates and follow his actions, there are two incidents, or series of incidents, in which the bishops, or at least a number of them, acted in concert, and in each case confusions and omissions are noticeable in all printed accounts. The first series is that of the various appeals made to Rome, the second is that of the anti-papal *démarches* made by the king. In what follows, after an account of the embassy to Sens, the question of appeals will be treated next; then will follow a review of the action of the bishops, with a somewhat detailed study of Gilbert Foliot; then the king's anti-papal actions will be considered; and, last of all, the clash between the three prelates and Thomas immediately preceding his murder.

(ii)

The deputation chosen at Northampton to present the case against Thomas to the Pope was not, as has sometimes been stated, intended to prosecute the appeal of the bishops. The group of envoys from England, among whom were the Earl of Arundel and other lay magnates, had as its nucleus the trio of associates Roger of York, Gilbert of London and Hilary of Chichester; to these were added the canonist, Bartholomew of Exeter and, for a reason which does not appear, Roger of Worcester.[1] They had as their business to inform the Count of Flanders, the King of France and the Pope of Henry's position and the archbishop's treachery, and to persuade the Pope to deliver

[1] The full list is given by Guernes, 2246-53, and I Anon, IV 61. Besides the five prelates, there were: the Earl of Arundel; Reginald of S Valéry, one of the signatories at Clarendon; Hugh de Gundeville, later sheriff of Hants, Northants and Devon, and one of the governors of the young king (W. Cant., I 108); Henry Fitzgerald, royal chamberlain, baron of the Exchequer and judge itinerant; Guy le Roux, dean of Waltham, baron of the Exchequer, and judge itinerant; John of Oxford; and Richard of Ilchester. Their commission was to demand a summary condemnation of Thomas or, failing this, a legate to hear the case (i.e., the appeal) in England (H. Bosham, III 336).

summary judgment on Thomas; they were not to stay more than three days at the Curia, and were not to await the arrival of Archbishop Thomas or take part in a suit against him.[1] In the sequel, they obeyed their instructions to the letter.

They reached Sens a few hours before Herbert of Bosham and other clerks sent ahead by the archbishop, and saw the Pope in private. On the following day the party was received in full consistory. Herbert of Bosham, who was present, gives a full account of the proceedings, and another biographer, Alan of Tewkesbury, gives a narrative which, while doubtful in detail, agrees well enough with Herbert.[2] All the bishops spoke, save Roger of Worcester, who was not backward on other occasions when he felt strongly. All were careful to stress the orthodoxy of Henry, and his amenability to correction, and represented the archbishop as an ambitious and impossible man.[3] Foliot, we are told, was the first to speak: he gave a description of the behaviour of Thomas at Northampton, and broke into a more general recrimination. 'Gently, brother', interrupted the Pope. 'Holy father, I will be gentle with him', answered Foliot. 'It was yourself, not him, whom you seemed to be harming',

[1] H. Bosham, III 336-7; W. FitzStephen, III 74: 'ut eis jussum fuerat ultra triduum non morari in curia, neque archiepiscopum ad causas prosequendas exspectare.'

[2] Alan of Tewkesbury, so far from being present, was at this time in Italy. His credentials, however, were considerable; *v. supra*, p. 72 n. 1.

[3] The statement of W. FitzStephen (III 73) that while before the Curia: 'nullus omnino contra personam archiepiscopi, vel quod eam vel causam regis et ejus tangeret, aliquid dicebat', cannot be accepted. It is contradicted by all the other biographers, including Herbert of Bosham, who was present, and who wrote an account almost immediately to a friend, while FitzStephen was in England at the time and may have heard only the version given out for propaganda.

replied Alexander.[1] This shook the bishop, and he soon gave place to the fluent Hilary.[2] The bishop of Chichester was an old *curialis* and no doubt was on his mettle, while his former colleagues, who knew his foibles, listened with a critical ear. He launched into a denunciation of the archbishop: 'Et certe' (he exclaimed) 'virum tantae auctoritatis non decuit, nec oportuit, nec aliquando oportuebat, insuper sui si saperent non oportuerunt . . .' At this point his solecisms were drowned in the laughter of the assembled cardinals and clerks, and a voice was heard to call: 'He's made the wrong port'.[3] Roger of York intervened to rescue the case, and in a short and sober speech demanded the Pope's intervention; he was followed by Bartholomew of Exeter, who in a few words asked for legates to hear and decide the case in England. Alexander was in a dilemma. The envoys had pressed him hard in private with veiled threats, and had made good use among the cardinals of the

---

[1] According to Alan of Tewkesbury (II 338) Foliot had applied to the archbishop the words of Scripture: 'Fugit impius nemine persequente' (Prov. 28.1). The Pope interrupted: ' "Parce", inquit "frater". Et Lundoniensis, "Domine, parcam ei". Et dominus papa, "Non dico, frater, quod parcas ei, sed tibi".'

[2] Hilary's grammatical misfortunes are retailed with greater or less detail by most of the biographers. Alan (II 338-9), who is followed in the text, has the fullest account, which may well represent an embroidered version of the incident, but that something remarkable took place is vouched for by Herbert of Bosham, who was present, not only in his life of the archbishop (III 336), but in a private letter written within a few months of the event (V 341-2): 'Quorum [*sc.* nuntiorum] unus, qui abstemius est . . . imperatum est a summo patrum patre ut parcius ageret . . . Alius vero, qui maxime gloriari solet de humanae sapientiae verbis, mox ut est locutus, nec vox erat ei nec sensus', &c.

[3] Alan, II 339: 'Unus prorumpens in vocem, "Male", inquit, "tandem venisti ad portum".'

funds they had brought from England. Yet he knew that to send the archbishop back to face Henry in his island kingdom was equivalent to telling a manacled prisoner in a dark cell to settle matters with his gaoler. In the event he stood firm. He would hear the archbishop and then decide. To a further request for legates he answered that he would not give his glory to another. The envoys returned and reported to the king about Christmastide at Marlborough. Henry immediately expelled all the archbishop's relatives and clerks from England. It was the end of a chapter: if the comparison is permissible we may say that as in the autumn of 1914 after the Marne armies in the West lost their mobility in trench warfare, so, after the dramatic turns of fortune in 1164, there ensued six years of desultory warfare which is almost as tedious and as difficult to follow.

(iii)

Before considering the parts played by individual bishops it will be well to glance at the occasions on which all or a number acted together, particularly in appeals to Rome. These appeals have given rise to numerous confusions. They were in fact three in number: the appeal at Northampton in 1164; that after Vézelay in the summer of 1166, renewed in November 1167; and that shortly before and again shortly after the excommunication of Gilbert Foliot in the spring of 1169.

The appeal made at Northampton on October 13th, 1164, was in the nature of a counter-move to safeguard the bishops while acting against their metropolitan, and was based on the plea that he had forsworn himself and had caused the bishops to fail in their feudal duties towards the king. When the embassy to Sens had failed, nothing further was done, and it is not till the following August that we find Foliot asking the king what is to be done about the appeal, which is now nearing its term.[1] No reply is preserved, and there is no mention in any of the sources of the appeal being heard; a document, however, appears among the papal letters bearing no date which annuls the sentences passed on the archbishop at Northampton specifically on the ground that an inferior and a subject cannot judge a superior, least of all a spiritual superior.[2] Whether or no this decision had any connection with the appeal, it tacitly ignored the existence of feudal obligations such as had been pleaded by the bishops, and would certainly, taken in conjunction with the papal condemnation of many of the articles of Clarendon, have cut the foothold from under the bishops, who would have been left without a case.

The second appeal was made on June 24th, 1166, as a direct consequence of the Vézelay excommunications; the motives alleged were the apprehensions roused by the uncanonical suspension of the bishop of Salisbury and the fear that the archbishop would proceed to more general measures, including an excommunication of the king. The appeal was made by at least four different parties: the bishops and clergy of England; the clergy of the Canterbury province; Jocelin of Salisbury; and the chapter of Sarum. Ascension Day in the following year (18th May, 1167) was fixed as the term.[3] This appeal was ostensibly

---

[1] V 203. 'De caetero dies instat quem appellationi ad dominum papam factae praefiximus; de qua prosequenda necesse est nobis ut voluntatem vestram et consilium amodo certius agnoscamus'.

[2] V 178-9.

[3] V 403-16. Normally an appeal had to be carried to court within a year, cf. decretal of Alexander III to the archbishop of Rheims, *Decret. Greg.* IX, Lib. II tit. xxviii, c.v. 'Annus indulgetur aut ex necessaria et evidenti causa biennium'.

made by all the bishops, but only three had in fact set their seals to it; they were the bishops of London, Winchester and Hereford.[1] It was followed shortly by the letters of the bishops and higher clergy (July 6th), presumably composed at their meeting at Northampton,[2] and these in their turn were followed by the exchange of letters between the archbishop and Gilbert Foliot, of which something will be said later. The king's immediate reaction was to precipitate a crisis with Alexander, and this probably accounted for the wide concessions temporarily granted (or promised) to Henry and conveyed to England by John of Oxford, whose opportune meeting with Foliot and Robert of Hereford on their way to the archbishop caused the return home of those prelates. These negotiations with Henry may explain why the Pope took no formal recognition of the appeal till December 1st, 1166, when he announced the appointment of legates to judge and settle the whole affair.[3] This automatically suspended the appeal.

Almost a year later, the final meeting with the legates took place at Argentan. Gilbert Foliot delivered a violent speech against the archbishop and, since it was clear that the legates had failed to persuade Thomas and were unwilling to judge him, Foliot professed himself ready to abide by any legatine decision and then appealed in the

[1] John of Salisbury to Bartholomew of Exeter, VI 65: 'Signata est attestatio eorum, omnium quidem concepta nomine, sed trium dumtaxat episcoporum roborata sigillis; archisynagogi videlicet Londoniensis, et domini et amici mei, cui interim parco, episcopi Wintoniensis, et . . . episcopi Herefordensis'.

[2] Nicholas of Mont St Jacques to Archbishop Thomas, V 422. 'Concilium quoddam habituri sunt in octavis Apostolorum [i.e., July 6th, 1166] episcopi et omnes abbates apud Norhamtonam'. Cf. ibid., 449, where the assembly is noted as having taken place.

[3] VI 125.

name of all the bishops of England against all the archbishop's unjust actions, past and future (29th November, 1167), fixing the term of the appeal at Martinmas next (11th November, 1168).[1] The bishops of London, Salisbury, Worcester and Chichester were present at Argentan, but only London and Salisbury and (according to some authorities) Winchester are reported as having given their names to the appeal.[2] The appellants were formally released from their undertaking on 24th April, 1168, ostensibly as an act of grace to save them expense, but no doubt because they no longer wished to press their case, while the Pope was anxious to restore to the archbishop full control over his province.[3]

The remainder of the year 1168 was spent in negotiations, and the archbishop's hands were tied by the Pope, who was unwilling to let him proceed to extremes. At the beginning of the following Lent, however, his hands were freed. Foliot, rendered wary by past misfortunes, had long known

---

[1] Ecclesia Anglicana ad Thomam Cantuariensem archiepiscopum, VI 289-91.

[2] A friend to the archbishop, VI 272: 'Episcopus etiam Saresberiensis [*sc.* in addition to the bishop of London] in hac appellatione se posuit, et episcopus Wintoniensis'. The appeal, like the previous one, was made in the name of the clergy of England (VI 285-91). There is a difficulty in the appearance of Henry of Winchester, as there is no record of his being at Argentan. Roger of Worcester was there (VI 270), and the names of the two sees are often confused in the manuscripts. On the other hand, one manuscript reads *episcopum Wintoniensem*, i.e., Jocelin signed for Henry as well as himself. It does not seem possible to be certain what happened. John of Salisbury, it may be added, writing to Bartholomew of Exeter (VI 324), refers to this appeal as the *third*. Strictly speaking, however, it was a renewal of the *second*, i.e., that of 1166.

[3] VI 388-9. The papal letter reprimands the bishops severely.

what would happen when the archbishop could once more loose his shafts, and, without waiting for the blow to come, appealed to Rome, fixing the term for a year ahead.[1] The archbishop in any case denied the validity of an appeal *ad cautelam* against lawful authority, and on Palm Sunday, 1169, he excommunicated the bishop of London.[2]

The news crossed the Channel in advance of the letters, and Foliot's agitation was extreme. He called a council and then a synod of his diocese; he begged Bartholomew of Exeter to join with him in the recent appeal, while at the same time he warned the bishop (apparently in vain) to abstain from receiving from him the kiss of peace. He told his clergy that he had been excommunicated, but claimed that the formal notification had not been made and that in any case he, as bishop of London, who had never made profession to Canterbury, was exempt from the archbishop's jurisdiction. Meanwhile a watch was set on the ports to intercept the fateful letters, and the various dignitaries, such as the bishop himself, his dean, the bishop of Rochester and the prior of Canterbury, who might expect to find themselves unwillingly served upon, absented themselves from their usual addresses. On the other side of the Channel the archbishop was having considerable difficulty in finding a messenger willing to take the risk, and likely to escape the hazards, of serving the letters on Foliot. In the event a young man of resource presented himself, who accomplished his mission adroitly and dramatically, by putting the letters into the unsuspecting hands of the celebrant in St Paul's on Ascension Day, with a prohibition against continuing the Mass before they had been publicly read.

[1] VI 535-7
[2] VI 541

Foliot immediately called a meeting of his clergy, at which he defended his canonical position and once more alleged the independence of the see of London. At the end of the meeting all joined in an appeal to the Pope.[1] At the same time Foliot was tireless in himself writing, and urging others to write on his behalf, and a sheaf of testimonials went out from the religious houses of his diocese vouching for his excellence of character; the writers could not understand how such a peace-loving man could be accused of fomenting discord; as for opposing the archbishop, why, they have often heard the bishop say how absurd such a charge was.[2] A smaller but more pointed bundle of letters written in the contrary sense reached the Pope at the same time: the writers were continental prelates who sympathized with the exiles. Meanwhile the bishop of London, after some hesitation, decided to act as if the excommunication were valid, and a pathetic letter found its way to the Pope: the bishop is old, and had hoped to spend the years that remained to him in preparing for his end, assisted by Alexander. Now all this has happened, and he cannot even get to Rome to explain everything because enemies are lying in wait to catch him, promising themselves that he will be carrying the wealth of the city of London with him.[3] In the sequel, despite a letter from the king telling him to disregard his excommunication, Foliot embarked on a trip to Rome and proceeded as far as Milan, where he found letters from Alexander telling him that faculties to absolve him had been given to the archbishop of Rouen and

[1] W. FitzStephen, III 87-90. Letter to the archbishop, VI 603-7. Foliot himself gives the story of all his appeals in a letter to the Pope in 1170 (VII 296-7).

[2] VI 610-39.

[3] VII 76-7.

another. Foliot was effusive in his thanks, and eventually received absolution on Easter Day, 1170, from Rotrou of Rouen. He was not, however, to be long out of the toils, for a few weeks later he was present at the illicit coronation of the young king. This time the Pope was as eager to act as Archbishop Thomas, and it was the notice of Foliot's last excommunication, sent to him across the Channel a few hours ahead of the returning archbishop, that was to prove an essential link in the circumstances that led to the murder.

(iv)

With the flight of the archbishop from Northampton there vanished also the centre of gravity which during the previous two years had drawn together and bonded the English hierarchy. Henceforward each bishop acted as a unit, or joined in association with others as he saw fit, though throughout the years of exile the archbishop across the Channel remained a pole of attraction or repulsion. In considering the conduct of the prelates it will perhaps be well to group them differently from before, according as they tended to support, or to be opposed to, the archbishop. Five, indeed, need not be considered at all. The bishops of Durham and Lichfield-Coventry, for reasons which can be neither discovered nor surmised, remained entirely aloof, save for a single incident to be mentioned in its place. The bishops of Lincoln, Ely and Wells, all old men and invalids, pass silently away after years of apparent inactivity.[1] We are left, therefore, with the archbishop of York and nine bishops, and these may be divided very roughly into two

[1] Robert of Bath and Wells *ob*. 31st Aug., 1166; Robert of Lincoln, *ob*. 27th Dec., 1166; Nigel of Ely, *ob*. 30th May, 1169; Hilary of Chichester *ob*. 19th July, 1169.

groups, six on the whole friendly, and four inimical, to the archbishop of Canterbury.

WALTER OF ROCHESTER, though so closely bound by past and present associations to the see of Canterbury and its occupant, played an inconspicuous and unheroic part in the conflict. He was the recipient of one of John of Salisbury's many letters asking for help for Archbishop Thomas, but there is no evidence that he gave moral or material support of any kind.[1] On two occasions at least he took care to be absent when important decisions were pending; thus in the spring of 1169 he left Rochester to avoid being the recipient of Thomas's letter excommunicating Foliot,[2] and a few weeks later he had a diplomatic illness which prevented him from being present at a meeting called by the king to organize resistance.[3] He was, however, present at the coronation of the young king in 1170, and it is significant that in September of that year, when the Pope was dealing with Thomas's opponents, the bishop of Rochester was left to his discretion, as one who should have been more constant in his support.[4] Two months later, he was suspended by the Pope, but he is recorded as having gone out a day's journey to meet the returning archbishop on his triumphant progress to London.[5]

BARTHOLOMEW OF EXETER was one of the king's envoys to Sens in 1164, doubtless as a canonical expert, and there

[1] VI 349. Letter of John of Salisbury to Walter of Rochester.

[2] W. FitzStephen, III 89. 'Et prior Cantuariensis ab ecclesia recedit; episcopus Roffensis similiter'.

[3] W. Cant., I 57. 'Episcopus vero Roffensis, per simulatam, ut dicunt, infirmitatem, suam excusavit absentiam.'

[4] The reference to the bishop of Rochester is in the letter of the Pope to the archbishop, VII 357-8 (10th Oct., 1170); cf. *ibid.*, 363, 397.

[5] W. FitzStephen, III 122.

asked for legates—a request which may have been made from goodwill towards the archbishop. In any case, he continued to receive affectionate letters from his old friend and colleague, John of Salisbury, who in the summer of 1166 addressed to him one of the most brilliant of all his letters, in which, with a mixture of bitter sarcasm and solemn imprecation, he tore to shreds Foliot's letter in defence of the king.[1] On the same occasion he told Bartholomew that he would shortly receive a formal summons, of which he need take no notice, to join the exiled archbishop. A year later, in the summer of 1167, John writes more sharply to the bishop's archdeacon, Baldwin, the future abbot of Ford and archbishop of Canterbury.[2] Bartholomew, he tells him, has been a useless friend to his archbishop and will shortly find himself in an awkward predicament: the legates, against Thomas's wish and without full papal approval, have decided to absolve those excommunicated by Thomas, and Foliot and his friends have passed on the risky task of absolution to Bartholomew. He advises the bishop, if he cannot stave off the applicants, to get expressions of penance and other promises from them. Whatever he does, let Bartholomew avoid signing the appeal which the bishops are organizing, even if this means trouble with the king. He has twice joined the appellants and has been forgiven; a third time will be fatal. Two years later, in the spring of 1169, we have a glimpse of Bartholomew standing *quasi murus inexpugnabilis* in his refusal to join with Foliot in his appeal after excommunication, and receiving words of encouragement and advice from John.[3] Later in the year, when the king

[1] VI 62-71.
[2] VI 319-26.
[3] W. Cant., I 56; VII 57.

was enlisting support for his anti-papal measures, Bartholomew refused to agree and withdrew from the storm to a
monastery.[1] It seems clear that he was not concerned in the
absolution of Foliot in 1170,[2] and he was probably not
present at the coronation of the young Henry, for, though
included in the subsequent papal reproof, he was warmly
defended by the archbishop and escaped suspension.[3]
Bartholomew, then, for all his equivocal conduct, was
regarded throughout by the archbishop and John of Salisbury as a friend.

As a celebrated master of Paris, bound by no English
ties or past actions, and as one chosen and consecrated by
the archbishop with the support of the Pope, ROBERT OF
HEREFORD was expected to give firm support to his
metropolitan. For this reason he was ordered by Alexander
in June, 1165, to accompany the bishop of London on his
embassy of remonstrance to the king. The result was
disappointing, and the Pope told him so: Robert had
shattered the hopes raised by his election; he is putting

[1] VII 176; VI 606.

[2] W. FitzStephen, III 92, states that Rotrou of Rouen and
Bartholomew were given faculties to absolve Gilbert Foliot, and a
casual reader would gain the impression that both bishops took
part in the absolution, though FitzStephen implies that Foliot was
absolved while abroad, and there is no evidence that Bartholomew
was out of the country during this year. Actually, both the papal
bull and other documents in the *Materials* show considerable
uncertainty as to the second delegate, who appears in various
manuscripts as Bartholomew, Bernard of Nevers and Arnulf of
Lisieux. In fact, Rotrou acted alone in giving absolution (VII 276)
and it seems clear that the bishop of Nevers was his colleague with
faculties.

[3] VII 388. The words of W. FitzStephen (III 117) and H. Bosham
(III 458) are ambiguous, but it is hard to see why Bartholomew, if
present, should have escaped censure from Thomas.

human fear before the fear of God, and Alexander commands him to support his archbishop.[1] That the reproof was partly justified can be seen from the selection by the king of the bishop of Hereford as one of the committee charged to examine the constitutions of Clarendon and certify them as unexceptionable.[2] Nevertheless, in the spring of 1166 Robert, along with Roger of Worcester, received personal notification of Thomas's legation, as being particularly bound to the Holy See and to the archbishop.[3] This confidence was in part, at least, misplaced, for a well-informed friend in 1166 wrote to Thomas that even Hereford was among the bishops who accused him and were appealing against him.[4] This failure drew a characteristic letter from John of Salisbury. Not so long ago (he wrote) the bishop of Hereford seemed to be one who was to redeem Israel, and to those without learning he appeared learned; now, he accuses the archbishop of setting the church in a turmoil, whereas Thomas could justly retort: 'It is not I who have troubled Israel, but thou and thy father's house'. Do not men say that the bishop of Hereford is the guardian of his king? Shall we not, then, say to him: 'Art thou not a man? Wherefore then hast thou not guarded thy Lord the king?' When Robert of Melun, John continues in his letter to the archbishop, was a master in theology he despised money but was greedy of fame; we

---

[1] V 252 (Alexander III to Robert of Hereford: 'Humanum timorem timori Dei, quod tuam religionem non decuit, diceris proposuisse ... spe nostra in promotione tua quodammodo frustrari videamur'.

[2] V 287.

[3] V 344-6.

[4] V 422 (Nicholas of Mont St Jacques writing early in July, 1166): 'hoc pro certo sciatis quod episcopi vestri etiam Herefordensis contra vos dura loquuntur'.

must get some of his old colleagues to write and tell him what they think of him now. Accordingly we find the abbot and prior of St Victor in Paris remonstrating with him, and the archbishop rebuked him severely but still affectionately.[1] Despite this, Robert of Hereford is found in alliance with Foliot when the latter writes a protest in the name of the clergy, and John of Salisbury grows more bitter against one who appeared at one time to have the shadow of a name, if not a great one.[2] John had advised the archbishop to summon his colleagues out to him; Robert answered the call, when it came for the third time, and got as far as Southampton, where he was met by papal instructions forbidding him to cross. According to William FitzStephen this broke his heart; he certainly died soon after, early in 1167.[3]

ROGER OF WORCESTER, as the king's cousin and the spiritual son of the archbishop, could not escape from becoming involved in the conflict, even had his forceful and downright character allowed him to remain silent. He was a member of the embassy to Sens, possibly with friendly intentions towards Thomas; in any case, he remained silent in the Pope's presence. He was one of those summoned to join the archbishop, and though he did not immediately obey he fell out of favour for a time with Henry, and John of Salisbury exhorted him to stand firm.[4]

[1] V 456; VI 20.

[2] VI 16. 'Quid dicam de Herefordensi, nisi quod aliquamdiu etsi non magni, stetit tamen alicuius nominis umbra, antequam sciretur quis esset?'.

[3] VI 151; W. FitzStephen, III 87; 'altius indoluit et . . . in illa doloris vehementia etiam correptus infirmitate suffocatus efflavit extremum'.

[4] VI 109-11. In this letter John refers with gratitude to gifts which he, as an exile, had received from Roger.

He was not, however, regarded as an opponent by Thomas, who wrote to him affectionately reiterating his command that Roger should join him.[1] This after a time he did; obtaining permission to cross the seas for the sake of study, he first went to the king's court and was with the king at Argentan at the end of 1167.[2] John of Salisbury heard that he had criticized the archbishop of Canterbury for refusing to resign on condition that the king would give a guarantee for the liberties of the Church.[3] During the next few months he passed from the court to the arch-bishop and back again, and while with Henry steadfastly and successfully refused to be in the same building with the excommunicated Geoffrey Ridel. Finally the king ordered him home, and the Pope joined his command, though warning Roger against obedience to evil principles. It does not, however, appear that he returned, and Arch-bishop Thomas had recourse to him in 1169 to defend the Church against the machinations of Foliot immediately after the latter's excommunication. He was present at some of the negotiations in Normandy in the same year, and to him early in 1170 Thomas turned once more and exhorted him by every memory of his father and every motive of religion and honour to prevent the coronation of the young Henry by the archbishop of York; he was bidden to hand an enclosed papal letter to Archbishop Roger. A further letter on the same subject takes another line and forbids him to cross the Channel.[4] With whatever motive, Roger went to the coast, but was forbidden, as a friend of the exiled Thomas, to cross and was therefore not present at

[1] VI 193-4.
[2] VI 270.
[3] VI 317, 321.
[4] VII 258, 301.

the coronation. He once more stood manfully up to the king on this occasion.[1]

Though the biographer who asserts that he was seven years in exile with Archbishop Thomas is greatly exaggerating,[2] Roger was in fact the most loyal of all the bishops, and the one who showed least fear of the king. Yet even so his conduct, as has been seen, was on more than one occasion equivocal.

WILLIAM OF NORWICH remains out of sight for the greater part of the archbishop's time of exile. He was an old man and, if his contemporaries can be believed, a good man. No other bishop, indeed, receives such generous tribute from both Thomas and Gilbert Foliot. Although, along with the bishop of Chester, he received power from the legates of 1167 to absolve those excommunicated by the archbishop, there is no statement that he exercised the power, and he certainly incurred no blame from Thomas; John of Salisbury wrote to him for aid in 1168, and his language is unusually respectful.[3] When the bishop of London was excommunicated, William was the first to dissociate himself publicly from Foliot,[4] and in the same year, when the king attempted to secure a breach with the Pope and the archbishop, William of Norwich, after excommunicating Earl Hugh against the royal command, laid his pastoral staff on the altar and retired into his cathedral monastery. A year later he received from the archbishop a

[1] W. FitzStephen, III 104-6.

[2] Guernes, 2680. 'Set anz fu en eissil.' Cf. W. FitzStephen, III 86. Guernes has a particular affection for 'Le gentil et le buen Rogier' (4788).

[3] VI 344.

[4] VII 50. 'Et hoc quidem primus fecit venerabilis frater noster episcopus Norwicensis'. Cf. VII 176.

letter announcing the reconciliation at Fréteval and expressing the writer's earnest wish to see him again.[1] At the end of the year the wish is reiterated still more warmly; the archbishop thanks God for the example the bishop has given as an unshakable column of the house of God, and prays that he may see him before William departs this life.[2] They never met, and it was the bishop of Norwich who survived his metropolitan by three years.[3]

Of all the bishops friendly to Thomas, HENRY OF WINCHESTER is perhaps the most interesting in his movements. The archbishop and he had been on amicable terms ever since Henry's return, as several letters of uncertain but early date show; Henry had long forgotten or forgiven the check to his hopes that Theobald's servant had effected years ago. John of Salisbury likewise had a personal affection for him—so much so, indeed, that he forebore to criticize him for sealing the bishops' letter of 1166.[4] There is a slight uncertainty, as has been seen, whether or no he joined in the appeal from Argentan in 1167, but the balance of probability is that he did not.[5] He was, in any case, consistently regarded as a friend by the exiles, and when their fortunes were at a low ebb John of Salisbury wrote to him as one whose alms were the tale of all the churches; not content with this, he urged the archdeacon of Surrey to propose the archbishop as a deserving object of Henry's charity.[6] Henry responded generously, even though it led

---

[1] VII 344.

[2] VII 416. 'Benedictus Deus, qui in his diebus posuit vos columnam domus suae immobilem'. The bishop for his part wrote 'sanctissimo domino et patri Thomae' (VII 417).

[3] He died 17th January, 1174.

[4] VI 65. 'Domini et amici mei, cui interim parco'.

[5] v. supra, p. 98.

[6] VI 339, 342.

to accusations before the king,[1] and an undated letter of the
archbishop's thanks and praises in the warmest of terms his
dearest, most beloved father, the source of his episcopal
power, who among the innumerable graces of the Holy
Spirit has the precious gifts of counsel and fortitude
beyond all his contemporaries and compatriots.[2] Henry of
Winchester had, indeed, firmly refused to join the excommunicated Foliot in his appeal. Like Kent, he had a journey
shortly to go; a day was at hand, he said, when his own case
was to be heard at the most august of all tribunals; appeal to
a lower one was barred.[3] He suited his deeds to his words
by publishing the archbishop's sentence against Foliot, thus
earning another letter of warm thanks, and continued his
firm stand six months later when the king endeavoured to
extract the anti-papal oath. This last piece of resistance
elicited an almost lyrical congratulation from John of
Salisbury and from the archbishop, who warned him to be
equally firm in withstanding the proposal of Roger of
York to crown the young king.[4] The bishop of Winchester
did indeed keep clear of the ceremony, and when Thomas
returned to England it was to Henry that he turned for
counsel, with Henry that he was prepared to discuss the
case of the suspended bishops, and in his house at London
that he stayed when he attempted to pay his respects to the
young king.[5] There is something very affecting in the
loyalty of the old bishop, with such a wealth of memories
of the past, to the younger man who had risen from

[1] W. FitzStephen, III 106 (Bishop of Winchester helping exiles).

[2] VII 45-6.

[3] VII 47, 50, 57-8.

[4] VII 138, 176, 261.

[5] VII 405; W. FitzStephen, III 122.

nonentity to success and fame and tribulation during his long episcopate.

Of the group of four who formed the opposition to the archbishop HILARY OF CHICHESTER need not detain us. After his débâcle at Sens he disappears for a time, till in June, 1166, he is said to be assisting Foliot in organizing resistance to Archbishop Thomas, who names him as one of the three instigators of the trouble. Then silence falls again, till in 1169 Hilary is recorded as publishing the letters of excommunication of Foliot the day after receiving them.[1] As he died on 19th July, this may well have been one of his last public acts.

JOCELIN OF SALISBURY had not been among those who opposed the primate most bitterly at Northampton, nor was he of the party that went out to Sens. The matter that brought him into collision with Thomas and made of him one of the inner group of irreconcilables was quite accidental to the main issue. When the embassy to Sens failed to carry the archbishop's position at the rush, and when it was clear that Alexander III would give him considerable support, the king resolved to make full diplomatic use of the anti-papal schism which was still being nursed by the Emperor. He therefore sent two of his clerks to the Diet at Würzburg (Whitsun, 1165), who did in fact take some kind of oath of fidelity to the antipope. Soon after their return Henry, wishing to reward John of Oxford, one of the envoys concerned, conveyed to the bishop of Salisbury his wish that John should be elected to the vacant deanery of his cathedral. This was doubly irregular: first, because John of Oxford, by allying with the antipope, had himself become excommunicate; secondly, because several of the chapter of Salisbury, with whom lay the canonical election,

[1] VII 50.

were among the exiles with the archbishop. Their rights in the election had been safeguarded by a papal prohibition to proceed without their voices being heard, and when the news of the king's *démarche* was known, both Pope and archbishop ordered the bishop of Salisbury to refuse to accept John of Oxford.[1] He did so, however, acting, so his friends said, under duress, and with recollections of the losses he had suffered on a previous occasion when he had withstood the king. The archbishop, therefore, who had been appointed legate of England on April 24th, 1166, excommunicated John of Oxford on his own account at Vézelay and shortly after suspended the bishop and ordered him to come personally to submit and be absolved.[2] His enemies maintained that this vigorous action was Thomas's revenge for the defection of the bishop's son, Reginald, who had passed from the archbishop's service to become an agent of the king.[3]

Jocelin immediately appealed against his sentence, and he and his family did all they could to bring pressure to bear upon the archbishop. The letters written by John of Salisbury to the bishop, to his son Reginald the archdeacon, and to his brother Richard, bishop of Coutances, have been preserved, and they all tell the same tale.[4] John has done

[1] The most precise account is that of John of Salisbury (V 433). The election was annulled by Alexander III on 8th June, 1166 (V 375).

[2] V 397-9 (suspension of Jocelin); 346 (Alexander III pleads for him).

[3] There is an interesting passage in Guernes (ll. 2291-2320, ed. Walberg), preserved in a single manuscript, which gives details of the ambiguous behaviour of Reginald in 1164. Walberg, pp. 257-8, has a valuable note both on this and on Reginald FitzJocelin in general.

[4] VI 186-93 (John of Salisbury to Richard de Bohun, Reginald FitzJocelin and Jocelin himself.)

his best; he has plied Archbishop Thomas with fair words
and harsh, but has always received the answer that an
example must be made of such open disobedience; he can
therefore only counsel submission. This the bishop of
Salisbury was not prepared to make; his was not a strong
character, and he turned for support to the bishop of
London; henceforth he appears throughout as the close
associate of Foliot. He is found in 1167 corresponding
with him in Maine, welcoming his prodigal son, exchanging
somewhat heavy pleasantries on the subject with Gilbert
Foliot, with references to the fatted calf, and following the
counsel of Hilary of Chichester, who is against moving
from Le Mans to Argentan at the risk of exchanging good
wine with a body to it for beer.[1] To Argentan nevertheless
he went, and joined in the appeal there made. Jocelin
secured absolution on terms from the Pope in 1168, but
when, early in 1169, Foliot scented danger again, he wrote
to Jocelin that they were in the same boat and asked him
to join in another appeal. When the blow fell, Jocelin
was struck along with Foliot and, according to one of
Archbishop Thomas's informants, spoke rudely of his
archbishop.[2] Immediate action against him was, however,
delayed; Alexander III wrote a personal letter to the archbishop, recalling his own old friendship with Jocelin and
alleging the bishop's age and ill-health as excuses.[3] It would
seem, though it is nowhere stated, that he was absolved

[1] VI 268, 269. The editor of *Materials* identifies the prodigal of
these letters with Roger of Worcester, who had certainly joined the
king's court in France, but I cannot think this identification
plausible. The prodigal is Reginald FitzJocelin.

[2] VI 606. 'Si Buinardus archiepiscopus meus (vel stultus archiepiscopus meus) praecipit mihi aliquod facere quod facere non
debeam, nunquid faciam? Absit'.

[3] VI 568.

early in 1170 by Rotrou of Rouen. The respite was short, for the bishop of Salisbury was present at the coronation in 1170 and in the autumn of that year was reprimanded and suspended by the Pope. It was now the turn of the archbishop to plead, and he was, on arriving in England, anxious to be merciful.[1] Jocelin, however, clung to Foliot, and Foliot listened to Roger of York, and all three went out to Henry in Normandy at Christmas. This put Jocelin in an unfortunate position when news of the murder spread, and William, archbishop of Sens, is found clamouring for vengeance on him. His age and bad health, however, which had already stood him in good stead more than once, were accepted as preventing a journey to Rome, and he was allowed to send representatives to vouch for his innocence. In the event, he lived for another thirteen years.[2]

Roger of York, the old personal enemy of Thomas, was naturally one of the embassy to the Pope in 1164, and spoke briefly but bitterly, urging drastic action. Thereafter he appears seldom in the biographies and papal letters for some years. In 1169 he is recorded as refusing to allow the anti-papal oath to be administered to his subjects,[3] but early in the next year he took the fatal step of consenting to crown the young Henry, thus running contrary to papal prohibition and age-old tradition. The Pope in September issued letters of suspension and excommunication, but entrusted their publication to the discretion of the archbishop. When the latter had extracted from the king leave to move against those who had taken part in the coronation, and was himself about to cross the Channel, he forwarded the letters to the three prelates, who were found about to

---

[1] VII 387 (Thomas pleads for Jocelin).
[2] VII 481, 492. Jocelin died 18th Nov., 1184.
[3] W. FitzStephen, III 102.

embark on the opposite shore. They delayed their crossing and approached Thomas through emissaries, demanding revocation of the sentence. The archbishop replied that the sentence was the Pope's, not his, but at length agreed to grant absolution on condition that those absolved should have recourse also to Alexander. Roger of York refused, and stiffened his associates with the assurance that he still had treasure in plenty, which he would use to the last penny in the Curia.[1] The three therefore crossed to Henry, and were at court shortly before Christmas. It was later said that Roger worked upon the king's indignation and was the direct cause of the departure of the four knights, whom he further briefed for their encounter with the archbishop. Whatever the truth of this, Roger was required, and was willing, to disavow on oath any share in the murder; the value of such an oath will depend on the estimate of his character.[2] Alone among the bishops, he is never in the published correspondence addressed in friendly fashion by the archbishop of Canterbury.

(v)

In the controversy we are considering the bishop of London holds a place apart. He is the coryphaeus of the opposition to Archbishop Thomas. He stands, in a sense, alone. Save for Roger of York and Hilary of Chichester and, in the later years, Gilbert's *fidus Achates*, Jocelin of Salisbury, the other bishops, so far as we can see them, held an irregular course. Foliot alone, with his two associates, neither tacked nor veered. But his two associates are not his equals. Roger of York and Hilary were in their

[1] So W. FitzStephen, III 121. 'Confisus in thesauris dicebat aliquando se habere papam et regem in scriniis suis'.
[2] For Roger's absolution v. VII 499-502.

different ways men of great ability, but they were not great men, either morally or intellectually. With Foliot it is different. For many years he had been, in the eyes of his contemporaries, the leader of his order in intellectual and moral power; the impression of mental power and force of character strikes from all his recorded acts and words during the years of conflict; he stands, indeed, as the great critic of the policy and personality of Archbishop Thomas, and as such his actions and his opinions deserve serious scrutiny.

Soon after Gilbert Foliot had returned to England at the end of 1164 he was given the administration of Canterbury by the king, and for a short while enjoyed what was virtually the primacy.[1] Indeed, it was probably Henry's intention, which could not have been unknown to Foliot, that the latter should succeed to Canterbury as soon as Thomas had been removed by deprivation, resignation, or translation. Events, however, did not move to Henry's plan, and in November Alexander III, having confirmed Archbishop Thomas in his office, solemnly condemned a number of the Clarendon articles, and shortly after declared null and void all the sentences and penalties passed upon the archbishop at Northampton.[2]

We cannot say how soon these facts became known to the bishop of London, but as soon as he was acquainted with them he was in a difficult position, and when the

[1] Cf. letter (VI 66) from the king to Foliot in 1165: 'quod se, totum regnum suum, et causam quae inter ipsum et ecclesiam vertitur, ipsius tanquam patris et fidelissimi amici committebat arbitrio ... Et praecipit ut officiales sui ei in omnibus usquequaque obediant'. For Foliot's administration of the exiles' lands and churches cf. W. FitzStephen, III 81-2; also Thomas's description, VI 50.

[2] V 178; III 342.

prospect of his succeeding at Canterbury had disappeared out of the line of immediate vision, he fell into the distressing posture in which he remained for six years, endeavouring to serve two masters. He was, it must be remembered, a monk, who had heard the peremptory words of the Rule first as subject and then as prior and abbot, and learnt and preached the virtue of unthinking obedience. The difficulty was that his obedience was engaged to two powers, and that they were at variance. To do him justice, the bishop of London was by nature neither subservient nor a trimmer, but he could not bring himself to renounce the plenary spiritual authority of the Pope and metropolitan in his regard, while at the same time he was pledged to recognize the feudal authority of the king, whose adviser and confessor he was by papal appointment, and whose advocate he had become through force of circumstances. He was therefore driven to the expedient, of which he made a use so frequent as to become in a measure ridiculous even to his contemporaries,[1] of appealing against the past, present and future action of his archbishop without ever pressing the case to a judicial decision. Perhaps the best way to understand his attitude is to trace one or two of the conflicts of loyalties through which he passed.

Despite the events at Northampton and Sens, neither the Pope nor the archbishop regarded Foliot with hostility. Early in 1165 Alexander III addressed to him a letter of mingled rebuke and request, urging him to use his inflence to bring the king to reason.[2] This was followed up in the summer by a formal command to take Robert of Hereford with him and visit the king to urge him to revoke the constitutions. The commission was executed; Gilbert and Robert sought the king out in Shropshire and Wales, and

[1] VII 19.　　[2] V 42, 175.

Foliot in his letter following the visit shows clearly how he intended to act. After an earnest plea for gentleness towards Henry he threatens the Pope with a schism in the Church, with England following an antipope, and with a rival archbishop of Canterbury and bishop of London.[1] Concurrently with this, Foliot was being attacked on the other flank. He had been given charge by the king of the churches sequestrated from the archbishop's clerks and had, according to his own account, allowed the revenues to accumulate. He was now commanded by the Pope and the archbishop to hand these over entire to the exiled clerks.[2] In this strait he avoided obedience to the mandate by a new appeal, but begged the king to relieve him of the care of the churches for the future. At the same time he made a direct and bold appeal to the king against the vindictive treatment of some of the clerks. Matters, indeed, had not yet come to a crisis with the archbishop. The first extant letter from the exiled Thomas is a reproof, but a gentle, paternal one,[3] while about the same time John of Salisbury is found seeking Foliot's advocacy with the king. The Pope's good opinion, however, was decreasing by 1166, and he is found wondering whether Foliot's character really corresponds to his profession.[4] At midsummer the next crisis came.

When the archbishop became legate, the bishop of London was charged with the duty of acquainting his brother bishops of the fact, and a little later was instructed

[1] V 203-9.

[2] V 316-20, 343-4.

[3] V 283.

[4] V 294 (Alexander III to Foliot): 'Saepe nobis a plurimis ea de te proponuntur quae ... utique si veritate subsistunt ... et spem et opinionem quam de tua religione habebamus omnino subducunt'.

to pass round a circular letter from the archbishop, together
with the Vézelay excommunications of the king's agents
and the condemnation of the Clarendon decrees, as also to
see to the reinstatement of the archbishop's clerks who had
been deprived of their benefices. A papal mandate to this
effect was served on Foliot in St Paul's at Mass.[1] This was
a peculiarly awkward moment for the bishop of London,
and his letter to the king, more perhaps than any letter he
wrote, reveals his mind. Against a papal mandate, as he
bitterly remarks, he cannot appeal.[2] He begs the king to
allow him to carry out the Pope's commands, while telling
the bishops that if they find anything in the archbishop's
letter contrary to the customs of the realm, they may with
confidence appeal. Henry, it would appear, was not helpful.
His reaction was to threaten schism in no uncertain terms,
and to announce his intention of sending the bishop of
London to the Pope to demand the removal of Archbishop
Thomas, the revocation of all his acts, and the public
engagement of his successor in the papal presence to keep
for ever the ancestral customs. Failing satisfaction on all
these points, England's obedience was to be withdrawn.[3]
To lead such an embassy would have been for Foliot to
feel still more keenly the rack on which he was already
extended; actually, nothing apparently came of the proposal, though it was bruited abroad and known to the
archbishop.[4] Henry, however, seems to have forbidden the
promulgation of the archbishop's letters, for the latter is

---

[1] V 359.

[2] V 417-8 (Foliot to king): 'Nam quod auctoritas apostolica
praecipit, hoc appellatio non suspendit. Nec adversus ejus man-
datum ullum potest esse remedium.'

[3] V 428-9.

[4] VI 68-9. John of Salisbury's comments.

found urging Foliot to do his duty and placing his finger with absolute precision on the neuralgic spot—the acknowledged duty of obedience to Rome.[1] It was in this atmosphere that the bishops and clergy of England, under Foliot's leadership, appealed as a body against the archbishop, ostensibly as a preventive measure against an excommunication of the king, which was felt to be imminent.

Foliot, as is well known, followed home the appeal with his long manifesto, of which something will be said later. Even before the letter John of Salisbury had finally hardened against Foliot, and it was he who suggested that the obedience of the bishops might be brought to the test by summoning some of them out to France.[2] The archbishop took the advice and called out some at least. Among them was Foliot, who, true to his principles, began to move and had reached Southampton when he was met by John of Oxford on his way back from the Pope with a privilege which was interpreted as giving the king and bishops virtual exemption from the metropolitan. 'Now Thomas will no longer be my archbishop', Foliot is said to have exclaimed.[3] His bitter letter had indeed set a barrier between the two men which was never removed.

The appeal after Vézelay was accompanied by a short letter of justification, ostensibly a joint production of all the bishops; actually, as John of Salisbury immediately recognized, and as the archbishop thenceforward assumed, it came not only from the pen of Foliot, but reflected his very individual point of view. In it the archbishop is taken to

[1] VI 181-2.

[2] VI 18-9.

[3] VI 150-2. 'De caetero Thomas meus non erit archiepiscopus'. Cf. *ibid.*, 172-3.

task for his opposition to the king, who is represented as the embodiment of sweet reasonableness, desiring nothing more than to be told if and when he has been at fault. We are fortunate enough to have the comments of John of Salisbury on this. The archbishop had passed on to him the bishops' letter and he recognized at once, as he says, the hand of Achitophel, for, he adds in the words of the evangelist, even his very speech doth betray him.[1] In another letter, one of the most brilliant he ever wrote, John rallies his old friend, Bartholomew of Exeter, on the achievement of his Demosthenes, the leader of the synagogue of London, 'Heaven help us', he exclaims, 'what a nerve the man has! "We do not say (he quotes Foliot) that the king has never been at fault, but we do say that he considers it the sweetest of all tasks to listen to those who tell him he is wrong". Does he think that anyone in Europe will swallow this?' And John quotes the resounding climax of Horace's epistle, where the poet tells of the man who, once deceived in the streets by a bogus cripple, refuses to hear even the best authenticated tale of woe; the whole street begs the unfortunate to try his story elsewhere:

'Quaere peregrinum! vicinia rauca reclamat.'
Let somebody send for the marines![2]

---

[1] V 408-13. Cf. John of Salisbury to Thomas, VI 13 *seqq.* 'Litteras . . . diligentius relegens . . . nihil probabilius . . . potui opinari quam eas, consilio Achitophel . . . per manum Doech Idumaei . . . fuisse dictatas . . . Nonne stylus ipse convincit Achitophel et Doech, quorum spiritu plenus est [episcopus Londiniensis]? . . . Nam et loquela ejus ipsum manifestum facit'.

[2] VI 63. 'Mirantur et stupent omnes qui audiunt qua conscientia, qua impudentia, qua fronte, ausi fuistis asserere, &c. . . . Si fidem, quam non habet, desiderat scriba vester . . . exeundum est de orbe Latino, ne quoties haec praedicaverunt, Quaere peregrinum, vicinia rauca reclamat' Cf. Horace, *Epistles* I xvii, last line.

After receiving this letter, and hearing John's comments, the archbishop wrote a long answer, traversing the legality of the bishops' appeal and giving a long apologia of his own conduct with some pointed reflections upon that of the bishop of London. To this he added a shorter letter of severe rebuke to Gilbert himself, charging him, bitterly and not in the best taste, with personal cowardice.[1] Gilbert replied in a long and celebrated letter in which he went methodically over the whole story and launched a frontal attack upon his rival. The authenticity of this letter was questioned at the beginning of the last century by Lingard and others and formally impugned by the French biographer of the archbishop, Dom L'Huillier, sixty years ago. It is treated as frankly spurious—as a good example of the English humorous parody—by the most recent French historian of the controversy. There is, however, no valid reason for accepting this verdict. The arguments against authenticity are extremely slender, those for it are of great strength, and in such a case, where no contemporary adverse evidence exists, the *onus probandi* most certainly lies with the sceptics. A statement of the evidence will be found elsewhere; here its authenticity is accepted as proven and it will be used, as is indeed both permissible and necessary, as the most important piece of evidence of what was in Foliot's mind.[2]

The letter is long, and considered as an example of the writer's literary and intellectual powers it is Foliot's masterpiece. As a piece of rhetoric—as the presentation,

---

[1] V 490-512, 512-20. 'Sed dicis mihi, "Pater mi, de quibus me calumniaris, absolvam me paucis. Tunicae meae timeo". Verum est, fili mi, et nimis verum respondes, et ideo gladium non habes' (518).

[2] For a discussion of the authenticity of the letter, *v*. Appendix VII.

that is, of a case in the way best calculated to emphasize its strong points, to conceal its weaknesses, and to carry the reader along with eager attention to a climax of intellectual and emotional sympathy—it is perhaps the only composition that has survived from the twelfth century that can rival the well known letter of Bernard, the *Apologia ad Willelmum*. Bernard, indeed, as a literary artist is superior to Foliot; the abbot of Clairvaux commanded a style which transmutes every word he wrote; but Foliot had a far more complicated case, and one far less easy of presentation; it is the skill with which he masters his material and the startling effect of his changes from narrative to the enunciation of principle and from suave courtesy to pointed irony and then suddenly to cold hatred that holds our attention and compels our admiration. Though written and sent as a letter it is as an art-form, so to say, a speech—that is, its power and effect would be greatest upon a hearer who could not stop to consider or return to re-read, but who would be carried on by the necessity of giving attention to an unfolding speech. With a speech, as in a play, the hearer, if his attention is held and his emotions excited, cannot easily detect inconsistencies of argument or narrative, or even unfair assumptions.

Throughout the letter Foliot, by a succession of skilful touches, puts himself in the right on both sides of the party-wall of principle and policy. Thus when Thomas is weak and subservient to the king at Clarendon the bishops stand, unwavering and unterrified, against the royal wrath; when he is rebellious and unreasonable at Northampton they are prudent and far-sighted in bowing to the storm. Thomas was unreasonable in refusing to make excuse in the case of John the Marshal, uncanonical in his submission to the findings of the court. Thomas's appointment to

Canterbury was an indefensible and unspiritual abuse of royal power strangling the liberties of the Church, whereas the constitutions of Clarendon are a venerable legacy to which a pious king is clinging from a possibly mistaken sense of honour; Foliot would pray for martyrdom and welcome the executioner's sword if only there were a cause demanding it, while the archbishop is rushing to arms and brandishing a sword against the sacred head of royalty in senseless obstinacy.

These are, I think, not unfair as summaries of the argument, but they are so skilfully presented in the letter that the contradiction passes unnoticed at the first reading, and the reader's indignation is kindled against the archbishop both for his weakness and his strength. Equally skilful are the silences. Foliot represents the bishops at Clarendon as standing firm in line of battle while the archbishop sells the pass behind their backs; he says nothing of the divided counsels and of the pleading of some of his colleagues that broke Thomas's resolution.[1] Similarly, while the concession made at Clarendon is noted as a failure due to the archbishop's weakness, not a word is said of his repentance and penance. While the king is said, quite truly, to have issued orders safeguarding the archbishop's person and property after Northampton, and Foliot likens this to the love of David for Absalom,[2] he omits to tell us that this was a

[1] V 521-44, especially 528 (at Clarendon) 'his omnibus [sc. episcopis] percussor defuit, non hi virtuti...terga dedit dux militiae'.

[2] V 536. 'Nam ut in Absalonem... paterna pietas exclamavit, "Servate mihi puerum Absalon", sic ejus mandato', &c. Cf. letter of Henry II dated Northampton (V 134, 14th Oct., 1164 the final day of the council) to King Louis: 'ne hominem tantorum scelerum et proditorem infamem in regno vestro... esse permittatis... Immo... efficaciter me iuvetis ad dedecus meum ulciscendum de tanto inimico meo'.

piece of studied policy, probably recommended by himself, to satisfy canonical demands and thus impress the Pope and Europe, and he does not mention the letters sent by the same David to his sheriffs and bishops ordering the sequestration of the goods of the archbishop's clerks and relatives, nor the letter from Henry to Louis of France in which the archbishop is called a perjured and criminal traitor. As for Henry himself, whom the archbishop is attacking, Foliot had already pictured him as one so little affected by the world's glitter that he is leaving his pure and noble queen, and the sweet pledges of their union, to take up the cross, stripped of all, to follow his Lord. He is a king who thinks it a delightful task to mend his ways and to make satisfaction when corrected.[1]

Foliot's letter must be taken seriously, for it undoubtedly represents the common form of the case made against the archbishop. Briefly, then, it is as follows. Thomas, the worldly, unscrupulous chancellor, was elected against the wishes of the clergy at the king's command. Church and State had hitherto been working in peaceful harmony till the tactless mismanagement of the new archbishop set them by the ears, and the king was compelled to demand the observance of his ancient privileges. Despite this, all at Clarendon were united in refusal till the archbishop, taking counsel of nobody, suddenly turned in his tracks and compelled the rest to follow. Bad as that may have been, it at least spelt peace, and all hoped the clouds would soon blow

---

[1] V 540. 'Nunquid non ipse est quem dulcissima pignora, nobilissima conjunx et honesta . . . mundi quaeque pretiosa vix detinent, vix blandiendo persuadent, quin spretis omnibus post crucem suam portantem Dominum Jesum nudus exeat'. Reading this we are profoundly grateful to John of Salisbury for his 'Quaere peregrinum!'.

over. Instead, the archbishop, going back on his promise, tried to go abroad; foiled in this by the elements, he was nevertheless kindly received by the king, till once again he embroiled matters by his senseless refusal to attend the king's summons. Changing again, he gave way, but ruined the chances of peace by holding out on the point of checking his accounts, and by threatening the king with his cross and appealing to Rome. Finally, he fled secretly from his post and then from a safe refuge called upon his colleagues to be brave and see that the king did not get the Canterbury revenues. A loving archbishop, indeed, who would imperil his brethren for the sake of cash. And it is here that Foliot, with splendid art, startles us with a gleam of steel. 'Even the Jews, my father, spurned Judas when he came to them with the price of blood.'[1] But setting this aside, he continues, thus relaxing our emotions, let us look coolly at the real issue. There is no question of faith or morals at stake, simply a matter of a few old customs, and these not even invented by the present king. The obvious course would be to use prudence and moderation; instead, the archbishop has attacked an excellent and pious king who would long ago have abandoned his customs had he been treated with common courtesy. It is to put a stop to these flaws and starts and thunderings that the bishops have appealed to the Pope, confident that a gentle approach will settle all. And Foliot ends with a reminder that Christ set before us the example of a little child who bears no malice

---

[1] V 537. 'Nos igitur ad mortem qua fronte, pater, invitastis, quam vos et formidasse et fugisse indiciis tam manifestis toti mundo luce clarius ostendistis? . . . Et annui vestri reditus nunquid vobis tanti sunt ut fratrum vestrorum sanguine vobis hos velitis acquiri? At Juda reportante pecuniam, hanc Judaei respuerunt quoniam sanguinis esse pretium agnoverunt'.

but wins all hearts by its innocent charm, and the still more august example of the One who defended his very executioners. Let the archbishop act thus, and then our devout king, our dear lord, will grant everything that is asked of him.

To this letter the exiled archbishop, so far as we know, made no reply, but it is significant that when, after a long interval, he again has occasion to write to the bishop of London, it is always in a tone of cold censure, while John of Salisbury never again wrote to Gilbert while Thomas lived.

(vi)

While the major controversy was passing from one useless meeting to another a small private dispute in England, minimal in intrinsic importance, as Foliot bitterly remarked, but nevertheless posing the same crucial dilemma as the larger issue, had important repercussions both at the Curia and at Henry's court. The last of the anti-papal decrees of 1169, which gives the impression of being an afterthought or later addition, states that the bishops of London and Norwich were at the king's mercy through having excommunicated the Earl of Norfolk at the Pope's command and without the king's permission. This was the climax of a long story, of which the barest outline must suffice.

The Augustinian canons of Pentney,[1] a small and poor religious house in west Norfolk, had appealed to the Pope, alleging that they had been unjustly deprived of their property by Hugh Bigod, Earl of Norfolk. Meanwhile the king, acting on the principles of Clarendon, had examined the case and arranged what appeared to be an equitable

---

[1] The Pentney documents form a sequence, VI 543-562; cf. also VII 149.

exchange, which the prior accepted. His canons, however, would have none of it, and appealed again to the archbishop and the Pope, who ordered the bishop of London to excommunicate the earl. The latter succeeded in obtaining a respite, but on failing to carry out the restoration as commanded the earl again became liable to sentence, which Foliot was ordered to fulminate. The bishop of London consequently found himself impaled, not for the first or for the last time, on the horns of a dilemma, and it is noteworthy that his reaction was very similar to that exhibited by him in the larger conflict. He told his troubles to Cardinal William of Pavia, the legate. He is in a fix, he says;[1] he must either disobey the Pope or perjure himself and fail in duty to the king, and what good will it do the Pope either way? He is perfectly willing to be a martyr, given a good cause, but not for the sake of half-a-dozen wretched canons carrying on a slipshod existence at Pentney. The king is quite willing to settle the matter if the Pope will let him, while the earl is perfectly willing to obey papal judges-delegate, if only the king would permit this. The matter dragged on, and Foliot delayed action; it was only when he himself was excommunicated that he moved. By so doing he ran upon the other horn also, for he had contravened the constitutions of Clarendon and was at the king's

---

[1] VI 546. 'Sic nobis in arcto res est ... aut hinc inobedientiae (quod absit) periculum, aut apud dominum regem perjurii et non observatae fidelitatis opprobrium. Mallem episcopus non fuisse, quam horum alterutrum incurrisse! ... Si causa quidem esset ... gauderem utique in ... morte. Sed nunquid sex fratrum in Panteneia miserrime et absque omni et regulae et ordinis observatione victitantium causa tanti est?' The example of Fortinbras (as also the teaching in Matt. xxv 21) would have been lost on Foliot; this was not the first time he had expressed his readiness for martyrdom, given a good cause (cf. V 537).

mercy. This may well have been an additional motive for him to lend countenance to Roger of York at the coronation next spring.

(vii)

A confusion similar to that caused by the appeals has arisen from the scattered references to the various crises in the relations of Henry II with the papacy. These have been somewhat neglected by historians, perhaps even unduly so, partly because of the lack of precise information and partly from a feeling of uncertainty as to whether Henry's threats were an expression of his settled policy or mere bluff.

The first acute crisis occurred in 1165, when it had become clear that there was no probability that the demands of the king and the hostile bishops would be granted or that Archbishop Thomas would lose the see of Canterbury either by resignation or translation or deprivation. Henry therefore took advantage of the European situation and sent representatives to the assembly of May 23rd, 1165, at Würzburg, where they made some kind of undertaking on the king's behalf, on May 29th, to support the antipope Paschal and abjure Alexander III. There are several accounts of this from biassed sources, and the episode led to the excommunication of John of Oxford, with all its consequences.[1] Gilbert Foliot tacitly refers to it in a letter to the Pope written about the end of July. There is a real danger, he says, that England will abandon your allegiance, and though many of us may refuse to be separated from you,

---

[1] W. Cant., I 52-3; V 182-4 (letter of Emperor Frederick), 184-8 (a friend to Alexander III, cf. also 188-91), 191-4 (proclamation of the Emperor), 194-5 (Rotrou of Rouen contradicting accounts of Englishmen taking oath to antipope). In spite of *démentis* it is clear that the English envoys gave some sort of support. Cf. V 375, 399-400.

there will not be wanting someone to bow the knee to Baal and receive the pallium of Canterbury from the idol's (i.e. the antipope's) hand. There will be found, too, those who will occupy the seats of us bishops; many indeed are already enjoying their meal in advance.[1]

How far the danger was serious; how far Foliot thought it was serious; how far both he and Henry were employing bluff, must be left to our private decision and to our opinion of Foliot's sincerity—certainly if the danger was not serious he may reasonably be thought either simple or unscrupulous. In the event no more was heard of the threat save when Henry, while protecting John of Oxford, gave the *démenti* to any engagement his envoys might have made.[2]

The second crisis took place shortly after the Vézelay censures. On this occasion Henry went further, and a letter survives written to the schismatical archbishop of Cologne in which he says that he has long been waiting for a good occasion of abandoning Alexander III, and that now, with the assent of his barons and clergy, he is sending out the archbishop of York, the bishop of London and Richard de Luci to Rome to demand the deposition of Archbishop Thomas, and that the Pope shall swear to recognize the constitutions of Clarendon. Failing this, England will abandon allegiance to Alexander III. The archbishop is therefore asked to send Brother Ernoldus to Henry with a

[1] V 208 (Foliot to Alexander III): 'Si hic rei finis extiterit ut . . . vestris (quod absit!) mandatis ulterius Anglia non obediat . . . nec deerunt qui sedes nostras occupantes, et cathedras insidentes, ipsi [*sc.* antipapae] tota devotione mentis obediant. Jam multi praemasticant ad talia.' &c.

[2] VI 78 (Henry to Pope). This undated letter is probably of 1165.

safe-conduct through the Emperor's territory.[1] Ernoldus was sent to England, and both John of Salisbury and the exiled archbishop soon heard of the proposed embassy to Rome. Neither Roger nor Gilbert Foliot, however, made the journey, possibly because they wished to avoid contact with the Curia at the moment, and the envoy was John of Oxford, who, excommunicated though he was, successfully extracted from the Pope the personal exemption of the king from all episcopal jurisdiction, and the cessation of the jurisdiction of Archbishop Thomas over his suffragans pending the arrival and judgment of legates.[2] It was on this occasion that Foliot, reading the papal letters at Winchester, is said to have exclaimed with delight: 'Now Thomas will never again be my archbishop!'.

The third crisis threatened to be the most serious of all. The storm raised by the excommunication of Foliot in the spring of 1169 when Henry championed the resistance put up by the bishop of London, and the failure of all attempts at a reconciliation between the king and his archbishop in the autumn of the same year, caused Henry to fear that the tide of papal favour had turned decisively against him; it seemed clear that he himself was once more in danger of excommunication, and that an interdict might be launched against his realm. He therefore drew up a new series of constitutions, in part supplementing, and in part sharpening

---

[1] V 428 (Henry to archbishop of Cologne): 'Diu desideravi justam habere occasionem recedendi a papa Alexandro.' John of Salisbury alludes to this letter (VI 68): 'quam gloriosam, quam catholicam, quam piam!'.

[2] VI 68, 140, 142-3, 147, 150-3; also 598 (Henry II to Foliot): 'Audivi gravamen quod ille Thomas proditor et adversarius meus intulit in te'; 599 (Henry to Alexander III, asking him to annul the excommunications of Foliot and Jocelin of Salisbury).

and implementing, those promulgated at Clarendon.[1] Some of them aimed at preventing the introduction and promulgation of papal letters; others forbade any appeal to archbishop or pope, or the holding of any plea at their mandate; all English clerks abroad were recalled, and all goods of those favouring pope or archbishop were to be confiscated; Peter's pence were to go to the king. Finally, all over the age of fifteen throughout England were to swear to the observance of these decrees.

The immediate aim of all this was clearly to forestall or counter any measures of the Pope or archbishop directed against the king. If fully obeyed, the decrees would have cut England loose from the papacy almost as completely as did the measures of the Reformation Parliament. They were, however, purely negative; though Henry took to himself some of the income and a few of the administrative powers of the Pope, he did not either deny the Pope's spiritual authority as such or substitute the royal or any other authority for the papal headship. There is no hint or threat of an antipope or of a new hierarchy such as had been pictured by Foliot five years previously. On the other hand, it was not merely a blind and impetuous move made in

---

[1] There has been some confusion in the past as to the date of these decrees, but it seems clear that the year is 1169 and the date shortly before Oct. 9th. The decrees are given, with some variations, in the collection of letters (VII 147 *seqq.*), by W. Cant., I 53, by Gervase of Canterbury, I 214, and by Roger Hoveden, I 231. Gervase, who seems to have had access to an unabbreviated copy of the original, gives the operative opening date for the application of the decrees as 9th Oct.; W. Cant. (*loc. cit.*) gives his account of the matter immediately after a notice referring to 1165; W. FitzStephen (III 102), though his indications of date are vague, appears to relate the incident to 1169, and this is in every way an acceptable date. Cf. Stubbs's note in his Rolls Series edition of R. Hoveden *ad loc. cit.*

anger and without forethought. It was one more attempt to realize what Henry had been aiming at throughout his reign—a regional church enclosed within the ring-fence of the coast, under his personal control, administered by a hierarchy of his own appointing, amenable to his justice in civil and criminal cases, and to the courts christian in spiritual cases, with himself as final court of appeal, the whole being still in communion, subject to certain personal limitations, with Rome.

Such a scheme was in many ways unrealistic. It was in the first place not traditional, if tradition were allowed to go back beyond the Norman Conquest. It was indeed made up of elements deriving in part from the pre-Conquest monarchy, in part from the Conqueror's establishment, and in part from the settlement of Henry I, but it had no ancestry in the history of either Empire or Papacy. Secondly, it was out of harmony with what was most dynamic in the life of the Western Church of the age and with the great intellectual and administrative movements of the time. Faulty as might be some of the title-deeds put forward by the canonists, centralization, articulation and spiritual autonomy had been the authentic notes of the Roman tradition in every epoch when the papacy had been free and pure, and in the twelfth century the mental climate of Europe was favourable to their development. Thirdly, outside the realm of canon law or dogmatic tradition, the age was one of moral earnestness, of intellectual progress and of centralized organization. The new orders, monastic, eremitical and military, were international and highly centralized; the nascent universities, whence flowed the ideas, were equally cosmopolitan. It was from such centres, and from the papacy, that the sap was flowing. Even had Henry II combined the qualities of the Conqueror and

St Louis he could not, in 1170, have made England what it was in the days of Lanfranc, a self-contained and fruitful moral and cultural unit, and in fact he had neither the moral stature nor the desire to be a reformer.

Nevertheless, the moment was a critical one, and England might well have been soon in *de facto* schism. Geoffrey Ridel and Richard of Ilchester summoned the bishops to meet in London to accept the new decrees; none however appeared.[1] Gilbert Foliot was absent from the country on his travels seeking absolution, and the lead was taken by Henry of Winchester, who solemnly proclaimed his fidelity to Pope and archbishop. He was followed by Bartholomew of Exeter and William of Norwich, both of whom retired to monasteries to weather the storm, while the bishop of Chester, in the only glimpse caught of him during all these years, is seen retiring out of the reach of the royal officials into the Welsh mountains.[2] The oath was indeed widely administered to clergy and laity, the only prelate offering active opposition being, somewhat unexpectedly, Roger of York,[3] and Henry had thoughts of

[1] VII 175 (Thomas to his clerks): 'Misit nuper in Angliam [rex] Gaufridum Ridellum, ut torqueat personas ecclesiasticas, et ad inobedientiae crimen nefariis obliget sacramentis. Is cum Ricardo Pictavensi, &c. . . . sed nullus episcoporum vel abbatum . . . comparere voluit'.

[2] V 176. 'Cestrensis vero . . . secessit in illam partem episcopatus sui quam Walenses inhabitant'.

[3] W. FitzStephen, III 102: 'Rex . . . jurare facit omnem Angliam a laico duodenni vel quindecim annorum supra'. This seems to presuppose an extremely efficient governmental control, and no doubt should be loosely interpreted. FitzStephen continues: 'Hoc sacramentum apostasiae nobilis quaedam domina filia Baldewini de Reivers [Redvers] viriliter agens et zelum habens obedientiae Dei, neque juravit neque aliquem hominum suorum jurare permisit. Archiepiscopus Eboracensis similiter libere fecit . . . archiepiscopus

crossing to England and enforcing his will on the bishops. Nothing came of this, however, though he pursued his usual tactic of combined threat and negotiation, and sent an embassy to Rome to demand that one of the bishops should be given what amounted to primatial powers.[1] The archbishop sent from France a pastoral letter of rebuke and absolution, and it was clear that the tide of feeling was now flowing strongly for the Pope and Archbishop Thomas, who were working in harmony. It is indeed possible that the king might have been forced into an agreement wholly acceptable to the archbishop had not his move, largely inspired by fear, to crown his son not given a new turn to events. Fatal though it was in the long run to Henry's fortunes, it had immediate and accidental consequences favourable to him, for it put some of the most influential bishops once more in a false position *vis-à-vis* the Pope.

Historians have very generally seen in all these moves of Henry little more than the diplomatic exploitation of a difficult situation. Everything, indeed, tends to show that

---

[Thomas] ... missis clam litteris ... omnes qui inviti juraverant a sacramento absolutos pronunciavit'. Cf. W. Cant., I 55: 'Abjurante itaque populo, militibus proceribusque beati Petri successorem Alexandrum per vicos, per castella, per civitates, ab homine sene usque ad puerum duodennem', &c. Thomas's letter of absolution is VII 220-3.

[1] Cf. the letter of John of Salisbury to Baldwin, archdeacon of Exeter, probably written shortly before Easter, 1170 (VII 234-5): 'Jactitabatur tunc regis nuntios absolutionem episcopi Londiniensis et omnium aliorum obtinuisse, et quod archiepiscopo subtracta erat potestas animadvertendi in regem et terram suam, sive regni personas. Fama celebris est quod memoratus Cantuariensis archidiaconus [sc. Geoffrey Ridel] regi persuasit in Angliam transfretare, ut episcopos torqueat et clerum qui contra dominum papam et matrem suam Cantuariensem ecclesiam jurare noluerunt'.

Henry, whose capable and in many ways realistic mind kept him within the bounds of the immediately possible, was unwilling to break with Alexander III until perfectly sure of his own position. Nevertheless, the decrees of 1169 are a carefully devised and logical complement of the constitutions of Clarendon, which had remained in the forefront of all negotiations, and it is hard to resist the conclusion that Henry, and the able administrators who surrounded him and who were at this very moment pursuing with such tenacity the organization of justice and government, had a programme before their eyes which they never abandoned, and which was produced and developed whenever circumstances seemed propitious—the programme of the regional church, under the king's personal control. On this occasion, in 1169, the scheme foundered on the opposition, all but unanimous, of the bishops.

(viii)

The rift between the bishops of England and their metropolitan, which had begun at Clarendon and had continued for six years, was destined in its final manifestation to be a remote cause of the consummation of the archbishop's career. The coronation of the young king Henry, which took place on June 14th, 1170, was performed by Roger of York, assisted by Gilbert Foliot, Jocelin of Salisbury and Walter of Rochester, in the presence of some, though not all, of the other bishops. Of those still surviving, Rochester, Chester and Durham were certainly present,[1] but it would seem that Bartholomew of Exeter,

---

[1] These are the bishops named in the two papal letters of suspension, 16th Sept., 1170 (VII 360, 364). Bartholomew of Exeter is mentioned there as present, but is excused by the archbishop (VII 388) presumably as absent.

William of Norwich and Henry of Winchester were away. The act was a challenge to the traditional claims of Canterbury, and the Pope was from the first as indignant as the archbishop. On September 10th Alexander issued letters suspending Roger of York and all who had taken oath to observe the evil customs of the realm; Foliot and Jocelin were to relapse into the excommunication from which they had recently emerged, and Walter of Rochester was left to the discretion of Archbishop Thomas.[1] These sentences were not fulminated, but a letter a month later authorized Thomas to hold or publish them as he saw fit.[2] The archbishop, unwilling to ruin the chances of a peaceful return by a direct and new controversy with the king, wrote to the Pope asking that Henry might be left uncensured, and that he might be sent three separate letters, to publish at his discretion, the first suspending Roger of York, the second excommunicating London and Salisbury, and the third suspending the other prelates.[3] He particularly requested that Bartholomew of Exeter—about whose presence at the coronation the sources disagree—should not be included among the censured. Alexander duly (November 24th) complied with this request, though it is doubtful whether his letters reached Canterbury before the murder.[4]

It is not wholly clear why the returning archbishop decided to use the instruments in his possession before he landed in England. When at Witsand, he heard that the three incriminated prelates were waiting to take ship on the opposite coast. He knew they were going away from him to the king in Normandy at the very moment when a

[1] VII 357 (Alexander III to Thomas, Sept. 10th).
[2] VII 382 (the same to the same; 13th Oct.).
[3] VII 384-9.
[4] VII 397.

reconciliation was having its effect; he knew also that they were going precisely with the intention of assisting at a number of episcopal elections to vacant sees[1]—another flagrant violation of his rights and a direct reassertion of one of the obnoxious constitutions of Clarendon. Whatever his reason—and whatever its wisdom—the archbishop sent the papal letter across the Channel before embarking, and was delighted to hear that it had been received and acknowledged. The prelates waited at the coast, and sent to the archbishop at Canterbury a request for absolution, emphasizing the incongruity of penal measures with a peaceful return. Thomas replied that the sentences were the Pope's, not his; that he lacked jurisdiction to deal with the archbishop of York, but that in the case of his two suffragans, he was willing to absolve them if they would express their willingness to submit to the final decision of the Pope and to accomplish what penance might be enjoined. The biographers are agreed that Foliot and Jocelin were for accepting these conditions.[2] Had they done so, the course of church history in England might have been different. In the sequel, they were overborne by Roger of York, who had no mind to be left alone, and who engaged himself to exhaust the considerable treasure of York in prosecuting the case at the Curia. To his arguments Foliot gave way, and the bishops went on their way to Henry. It was their account of the high-handed action of the arch-

[1] John of Salisbury writes (VII 409) that Roger of York and Gilbert Foliot had attempted at the last moment to prevent Thomas's return, and were making arrangements for the episcopal elections. The archbishop heard of this through friends (*ibid.*, 410), and his action against them was his direct counter-move—'conatus eorum via qua potuit elisit'. Cf. H. Bosham, III 477.

[2] John of Salisbury has this in a letter written before the murder (VII 412) and it is repeated by almost all the biographers.

bishop, and in particular the vindictive bitterness of Roger, that worked upon the king and led to the excess of fury in which he demanded riddance of the archbishop. For this, if common talk was true, Roger of York was largely responsible, and he had to go to considerable trouble in exculpating himself on oath from having incited the king to take action.

When the four knights arrived at Canterbury on December 29th, it was the absolution of the bishops that they demanded with persistence, both in the archbishop's hall and in the cathedral; it was the refusal of their demand, as being against justice and papal authority, that was the immediate occasion of the murder. Thus, the archbishop's words of seven years before—'the sons of my mother have fought against me.'—were fulfilled to the letter, although when he died at Canterbury the only colleagues within a hundred miles or so were the harmless Walter of Rochester and the invalid and well-wishing Henry of Winchester.

CHAPTER V

POLICY AND PRINCIPLES

(i)

BEFORE we take our leave of the episcopal colleagues of Archbishop Thomas, it may be of interest to consider how far they differed from their chief in their judgment of the principles at stake and of the policy to be adopted in the quarrel with the king. Our consideration of their actions and words before and during the controversy will perhaps have shown that, as a group, they had neither policy nor principles sharply defined or that, if they had, we have no means of discovering them. One exception, however, must be made. By a chain of circumstances which he could not have foreseen, but from which he made no effort to extricate himself, the bishop of London was placed in the position of king's man and rival leader to the archbishop; he had therefore perforce to adopt a policy and, being a man of mental power and literary ability, it was inevitable that he should feel called upon to formulate his principles.

As regards his policy for the Church in England, the breach with Thomas was complete. The archbishop, once he had repented of his adhesion to the constitutions of Clarendon, stood simply for the repeal of all those clauses which had been condemned by the Pope and for a free Church in the sense that the high-church post-Gregorians would have understood the phrase. The king must be brought to grant this, if necessary by the use of all the spiritual powers of coercion of which the archbishop and Pope disposed.

What, in distinction to this, was Foliot's view? The

reply must be that in theory he never explicitly maintained that the constitutions of Clarendon could be reconciled with the canons of the Church or the liberties of the English episcopate; he did, however, maintain that the quarrel was concerned purely with administrative method, and that the king was no innovator but simply asserting old customs of the realm, and that with tactful handling all would be well. On each of these three points, therefore, he differed from the archbishop, who would have maintained that some, at least, of the constitutions deprived the Church of freedom in essentials, that in view of this the argument from custom was of no force, and that in fact the king had an inflexible intention of increasing rather than of relaxing his hold. On the first two points it is scarcely for the historian to pronounce; he can only say that both parties, royal and papal, failed to realize that in an age of rapidly developing ideas and institutions a static view of any problem or institution was bound to prove unrealistic; he might also perhaps add that the spectacle of Foliot's perplexities, expedients and misfortunes would seem to show that, whatever might have been the best solution for one who wished to be a loyal supporter of Henry II while remaining an obedient son of the Pope, the bishop of London had not found it. On the third point—the argument, that is, that Henry, if appeased, would relinquish his obnoxious claims —all the events of the reign seem to prove that Archbishop Thomas's opinion was the more correct. Whether he used the most politic methods in translating this opinion into action is another matter.

So much—or, so little—for the difference in the field of policy. It need not necessarily have implied a difference in principle, but in fact it was an age when the doctrine of the relations of Church and State, *regnum* and *sacerdotium*, was being widely debated, and it would have been hard to take up a position for or against the offending constitutions without having some principles on which to rest, or with which to justify oneself.

In the course of the discussions at Clarendon and Northampton, two distinct problems confronted the parties concerned, though no one at the time, so it would seem, explicitly separated them in thought, still less endeavoured to disentangle them in debate. The first dominated the scene at Westminster and Clarendon, the second at Northampton, but both were potentially present throughout. The first was the ancient, classic issue of Church and State, *regnum* and *sacerdotium;* the ever-old, ever-new question as to the rights and powers of the temporal and spiritual authorities. The second, which came sharply to the fore at Northampton, but which has received far less notice from historians, is the problem of the relationship of the high ecclesiastics to the fully developed feudal state of the Anglo-Norman kingdom of which they were members. The organized feudal system, as has often been noted, had three essential characteristics: that of personal loyalty to the king; that of contractual relationship between vassal and lord; and that of solidarity among the tenants-in-chief which implied that they should share in and answer to all decisions of the king's Great Council as the highest feudal court of the land. This system, when applied to ecclesiastics, gave rise to problems somewhat similar to the cognate problems connected with the proprietary church and investiture; all were the legacy of an age in which institutions had developed in a number of Christian societies unregulated by any external supra-national or supra-regional authority. In north-western Europe before the end of the eleventh century neither the Pope nor the canon law were sufficiently powerful to control feudal institutions, and in England, at least, before the Conquest secular and ecclesiastical administration were so intertwined that there could be no collision, and so informally constituted that need had not yet been felt for safeguards.

But when the two sources of authority began to press their rival claims, and to demand a total obedience, as did the reformed papacy using the systematized canon law, and the Norman monarchy using rationalized feudal conventions, a bitter controversy was bound to ensue. At each stage of the Northampton dispute Archbishop Thomas came into collision with a feudal convention which had been always hitherto accepted implicitly or explicitly by generations of churchmen: the duty of the vassal to answer the summons to the lord's court and there to take part in the judgment or to obey the sentence as the case might be. No doubt at Northampton the issue was contaminated by the questions raised at Clarendon; no doubt, also, the patent animus of the king against the archbishop helped to take the minds of those present off the basic problem; but this problem remained, and Foliot perceived it and attempted to solve it. It was in essence the problem of reconciling feudal discipline with the requirements of canon law. It will perhaps be well to take the two issues—the wider ecclesiastical and the narrower feudal problems—separately in each of the opponents.

(ii)

On the wider issue three main questions came to the fore: the right of unrestricted recourse to the Apostolic See as the seat of supreme justice and discipline; the right of the spiritual power to use freely the spiritual weapons of coercion; the right of the king to judge and sentence criminous clerks. There was another important matter on which Henry had more than once shown his mind—the right of the Pope to issue privileges to his subjects without his cognizance—but this did not directly occur in the quarrel with the archbishop, though Thomas as chancellor had in the cases of Battle and St Albans, and probably elsewhere, heard and acquiesced, however unwillingly, in the royal pronouncements. We are not primarily concerned with the views or designs of either Henry or Thomas, but it is worth considering what measure of agreement there was between the archbishop and his colleagues on these points.

On the right of free intercourse there is no suggestion that any of the bishops would have disagreed with the archbishop's assertion of this as a basic and essential right of the higher clergy without which the international Church could not be governed. In practice, they were not greatly put out during the controversy by the decree of Clarendon on the subject, for Henry was so concerned throughout that his case and his prelates should stand well with the Pope that access to the Curia for one reason or another was easy.

On the second point, the right of excommunication, the bishops as a body might well have exclaimed with Oedipus that they (if the phrase may be permitted) were at the receiving end.[1] As the affair of Pentney showed, however, their interests also were at stake.

On the third matter, that of criminous clerks, much has been written, and it is now generally accepted that on this point Henry was more realistic than was his archbishop; that he was in fact standing for what had hitherto been a practice tolerated in the past by the Church and defensible

[1] Sophocles, *Oedipus Coloneus*, 266-7 : Τά γ' ἔργα μου Πεπονθότ' ἐστι μᾶλλον ἢ δεδρακότα.

even on canonical grounds. The archbishop's insistent application of the well-known canonical axiom *non bis in idipsum judicat Deus*,[1] though it carried the day for the time and was duly embodied in the decretals, was personal to him, and the claim may well be thought extravagant. No doubt, however, Thomas had his own schemes for reorganizing and strengthening the administration of criminal justice in the church courts, and the few indications that have been preserved suggest that had he been allowed a peaceful term of office, he might have shown himself as a great reformer and more remarkable than Lanfranc.[2] He certainly did not intend that convicted clerics should go unpunished; scourging and imprisonment were the measures he took against crimes far from heinous. But for the moment, and for our purpose, it is enough to note that the archbishop's position, however extreme, caused little difficulty to his colleagues. Though they required a certain amount of stiffening, they were ultimately prepared to make a stand with him here, and it was with justice that Foliot complained that the archbishop himself had abandoned an impregnable position. The unanimity of the hierarchy on this point was, indeed, so striking that the king was advised at Northampton not to raise this issue with the archbishop, lest by so doing he might once more unite the bishops and their primate.

(iii)

The narrower question, the amenability of the higher ecclesiastics to feudal obligations and courts, and to the

---

[1] For this text and its sources, *v.* Z. N. Brooke, *The English Church and the Papacy*, 205 and note 1.

[2] Cf. the cases given by Bosham, III 264-5.

royal control in general, has received less attention, but it came sharply to the fore at Northampton, and this raised the whole great question of the relations of Church and State. This issue, therefore, was debated at a high level more than once during the struggle.

As is familiar, three positions were taken up during the central period of the middle ages on this point by different groups. There was the old and so-called Gelasian theory of the two powers, spiritual and temporal, ordained by God for the two spheres of human life; there was the extreme papal position, adumbrated by Gregory VII but not fully developed before Innocent III, that the spiritual power stood to the temporal as the sun to the moon, and that the temporal power had been delegated by the popes to the Emperor or to monarchs either by a historical gift or by sufferance; and there was, thirdly, the imperial reaction to such claims, issuing in the counter-claim that the Emperor not only derived his power directly from God, but that his authority was in a sense superior to the spiritual. It will be remembered that the first—the Gelasian —view had by the twelfth century become somewhat modified and confused. Its original author had conceived the two powers as existing side by side in the world. Later, by an almost imperceptible and perhaps unconscious change, they were regarded as existing side by side in the Church—a far more difficult conception.

Archbishop Thomas, whatever his actions as chancellor may have been, strenuously maintained the autonomy of the spiritual power, though he was some time in presenting a perfectly lucid case. Thus one of his biographers tells us that even before Clarendon, on a public occasion when the king was present, the archbishop preached on the distinction of the two powers and extolled the immense superiority of the spiritual,[1] and Herbert of Bosham, when narrating the clash over criminous clerks, represents the archbishop as telling the king that the Church contained within herself two jurisdictions, each with its own sword and each autonomous in its own sphere, but that the spiritual is in a sense superior, as appointing kings and having jurisdiction over them.[2] Another biographer tells us that the archbishop refused to hear sentence pronounced against him, remarking that it would reverse all order if the sheep struck the shepherd, or the son the father, seeing that the priestly dignity is to the royal as gold is to lead.[3] That this was the common doctrine of the curial clerks, both at Rome and Canterbury, is seen from its appearance some six years previously in the speech of Hilary of Chichester in the Battle exemption suit. Christ, he said, set up two powers in the world, the spiritual and the material. Of these two the spiritual governed the whole Church, so that the king had no power to give or take away ecclesiastical office.[4] Hilary, however, went no further in defining the relative position of the two powers, or, if he did, the chronicler has confused and abbreviated his exposition. Archbishop Thomas, however, had a teacher still nearer at hand, for the doctrine of the superiority of the spiritual power to the temporal power had been

[1] I Anon., IV 22: 'Intelligensque [rex] quod dignitatem ecclesiasticam cuilibet excellentiae saeculari longe immensum praeferret, non aequo animo accepit'.

[2] Bosham, III 268: 'Unde privilegio ordinis et officii [clerici] terrenis regibus non subsunt sed praesunt, utpote qui reges constituunt'.

[3] Grim, II 398: 'Neque enim ita pretiosius est aurum plumbo, sicut sacerdotalis dignitas regia potestate'. The phrase derives ultimately from Pseudo-Ambrose, *De Dignitate Sacerdotali*, c. 2 (*P.L.* xvii col. 570).

[4] *Chronicon Monasterii de Bello* (Anglia Christiana Society), 90-1.

taught by John of Salisbury in a book which had been dedicated and sent to Thomas himself some years previously. It is nevertheless worth noting that no direct derivation of ideas from the *Policraticus* can be traced in the archbishop.

We know from his biographer that the exiled archbishop spent much time during his two years at Pontigny in studying canon law under the distinguished Piacenzan lawyer Lombardus, later cardinal and archbishop of Benevento.[1] It was then, probably, that he acquired his familiarity with Gratian. The fruits of this study are apparent in the second and third of the three letters addressed by him to the king early in the same year. The first letter had been a short and affectionate appeal, couched in moderate language. When no response was forthcoming, a longer and more severe and more doctrinal letter was despatched.[2] The archbishop begins by a statement on the jurisdiction of the monarch over the priesthood; members of the priestly class, he says, should be judged by their peers alone. The king has no right, as the son and the pupil, to judge his father and master. The writer then goes on to outline the relations of Church and State. All ecclesiastical matters are to be judged by the Church, not by the king; kings should follow the decrees of the Church, not set up their own power in opposition. And he quotes the passage of Gratian, already classic: 'There are two agencies by which the world is governed in the last resort; the sacred authority of bishops and the royal power. Of these, the weight of authority resting in the priestly class is as much the greater as is their responsibility, for they will have to

[1] Bosham, III 523: 'Hic discipulus [*sc.* Lumbardus] . . . magistrum in exsilio canones docuit'.

[2] Letter *Exspectans exspectavi*, V 269-78. Cf. Gratian, I xcvi 10.

give account of their care of kings at the last judgment.
You kings must know in very truth that you must depend
upon the judgment of priests; they cannot be bent to your
will'. And the archbishop ends by warning Henry that kings
may be excommunicated.

To this letter, also, there was no reply. In the third the
archbishop reiterated his claim with still greater amplitude
and emphasis.[1] The Church for which Christ died, pur-
chasing its liberty with His blood, is made up of two orders,
clergy and people. Among the people are counted kings,
princes and potentates of every rank. Now it is certain that
kings derive their power from the Church not the Church
its power from them; it is therefore not the king's task or
right to order bishops to excommunicate or absolve, to hale
clerks to secular courts, to judge of churches and tithes, to
forbid bishops to try cases of perjury and to do all else that
is written in the so-called ancestral customs of the realm.
Let the king remember his profession at Westminster,
when he promised the Church her freedom. The same
doctrine is put out in a letter written shortly afterwards to
Gilbert Foliot, in which Thomas tells him to make it clear
to the king that Christ has ordained two powers, the one
pre-eminent and worthy of all possible reverence, the other
with temporal authority to use in the service of the
spiritual power.[2] The king therefore is not to presume to
judge those who are his judges.

It will be seen that the archbishop has gone far beyond
the Gelasian doctrine, and his thought, though not his
language, is very similar to that in a well known passage in
John of Salisbury's *Policraticus*.

[1] Letter *Desiderio desideravi*, V 278-82.
[2] V 518-9: 'Unam [potestatem] cui potentiam concessit, alteram
cui reverentiam exhiberi voluit'.

(iv)

In all these utterances and letters, the archbishop studiously lifted the controversy on to the high level of doctrinal and canonical theory, where it might meet and mingle with the great Gregorian controversy of the previous century. There was, however, a more immediate issue on the lower level of feudal practice. This had come up suddenly and clearly at Northampton, when the king's feudal court passed sentence against the archbishop on a purely feudal issue, and it seems clear that on that occasion Thomas was unprepared and had no considered defence to hand. He began therefore by defying the king; then he yielded, and then, when yielding failed to appease, he lifted resistance to a higher pitch, alleging that the son, the subject and the lesser could not judge the father, the master and the superior. This, as we have just seen, was the theme of his later utterances on the point, and was taken up by the Pope. This, however, did not really meet the case as an adequate answer; rather, it begged the question by assuming that feudal relationships of all kinds were non-existent; a further explanation therefore seemed to be called for, even at Northampton. The archbishop consequently based his reply on two arguments: first, that what was given to the Church was given in pure alms, without conditions of tenure; and secondly, that the occupant of a see for the time being was not the owner but the steward, and that the property belonged neither to him nor to the king, but to the Church, that is, to God.[1] This argument has been treated as captious, if not positively dishonest; it was certainly shocking to feudal ears and had not been held in any recognizable form by Thomas himself in earlier years. Moreover, on a short view it was demonstrably bad history.

[1] Will Cant., I 39; Grim, II 398.

Since the Conquest the bishops and old abbeys had been consistently treated as baronies and fees held in chief of the king by a tenant who did homage and was bound to military service and the equivalent of feudal dues. Yet to some extent, at least, the archbishop had history on his side on a longer view. The property of the Church in England before the Conquest, though deriving in large part from royal gifts, was in fact regarded as belonging solely to the church concerned or to its patron saint, not to the king or the bishop. Gifts to the Church, all over Europe, had originally been made as gifts to God; it was only at a particular time and in particular regions, and in a crucial stage of semi-organized society, that they had come to be regarded as implying contractual relations. Regarded thus, the archbishop's answer was a genuine and true solution. He had been suddenly called to face a real problem—the dual capacity of the bishop as father in God and spiritual vassal, with its corollary that an unjust sentence passed upon an individual in the latter capacity might deprive him of all material possessions in the former, and he had cut the knot by denying personal ownership of Church property. The feudal problem was not a new one; it had been posed eighty years before by William of St Carilef, and on that occasion Archbishop Lanfranc and the king were in agreement that the bishop as a feudal vassal was amenable to the king's jurisdiction. Since then a heroic attempt to escape from the dilemma in high politics had been made by Pascal II with his proposal that the Church should surrender the regalia altogether. More recently still, a very justifiable attack on the family group at Salisbury, Lincoln and Ely had been foiled by the other bishops, jealous of their order's privileges. In normal times the dilemma in its extreme form, like its correlative, the papal claim to the right of deposition, could be avoided by tactful handling and a sense of common interest. Now, however, it had become a vital issue between two opponents of stubborn will.

It was, therefore, with this issue—the practical, feudal one broadening into the high ecclesiastical claim—that Gilbert Foliot, as king's advocate and leader of the opposition to the archbishop, had to deal in his indictment of the primate. His answer, as one might expect, is a cautious and moderate one.[1] On the issue of Church and State he is careful to put forward a view which, while orthodox and traditional, does not carry with it any dangerous implications. There are two powers, he says, ordained of God, the priesthood and the kingship. Each is in one respect superior to the other and can, as the fathers teach, in some respects be judged by the other.[2] Thus each may be in turn judge and defendant. Now the Church holds some things by divine right, others by human. Holy orders, and the powers and rights deriving therefrom, are purely spiritual, and only the Church can deal with such things. Here every priest is as such above any king, who is his son and disciple. If the king sin, the Church can judge him. And there are also material things which the Church holds by divine right, such as offerings, with which the king has no right to meddle. But the Church has also many material things, such as lands and wealth, given her by kings and laymen. And here Foliot, without emphasizing the transition, begins to face the practical issue of Northampton. Every giver, he says, can attach a condition to his gift and to these

---

[1] This is in the letter *Multiplicem*, V 532-3.

[2] V 534-5: 'Cum sit igitur a Deo potestas gemina, hinc sacerdotalis, hinc regia, utramque secundum quid praeesse alteri et ab altera secundum quid posse judicari patrum auctoritates confirmant'.

gifts of land conditions of homage and military service have been attached by the king; hence the Church serves both God and king, and its prelates are governed by two authorities, the one divinely conferred which regulates them as bishops, the other which comes from the king and affects them as barons. Hence the Church has power of judgment along with the king, and bishops may be obliged to assist the king in examination and judgment. Moreover when they thus act, purely ecclesiastical distinctions of rank disappear; in the things of God there is a distinction between higher and lower prelacy, but as feudatories all are equal. Therefore there is no absurdity in bishops judging their metropolitan. Nor is it strange that a spiritual father should be condemned by his son, when it is clear that the son is temporal lord of his spiritual father, from whom he has received homage.

In this exposition, which is in many ways a sober and statesmanlike one, Foliot clearly adopts, in a way that Archbishop Thomas did not, the traditional Gelasian doctrine of the two co-ordinate powers. What is personal in his exposition is the inclusion within the competence of the temporal power of all the complex of feudal obligations and loyalties that were undreamed of in the age of Gelasius. Its fatal weakness as a theory is that while it preserves, so far at least as words go, the independence of the two powers, it fails to keep separate, as Gelasius had done at least by implication, the subjects of those powers.

Unsatisfactory as this theory may appear, the original responsibility for it must not be attributed to Foliot either for praise or for blame. In its main lines it follows exactly the train of thought pursued by the reforming German ecclesiastic Gerhoh of Reichersberg, especially as developed in his treatises *De Novitatibus hujus temporis* (1155-6) and

De Investigatione Antichristi (1161-2).[1] It will be remembered that the expedient devised by some of the bishops for escaping from the impasse at Northampton was likewise an application of Gerhoh's doctrine—a circumstance that points to Foliot as its author.

One last point may be noted for comparison between the two adversaries. Both Thomas and Foliot refer to the English coronation ceremony with its multiple anointings, but there is an interesting difference in the conclusions which they draw. According to the archbishop the king has received his authority from the Church by the sacrament of anointing and by the investiture with the sword, given him to control the Church's enemies. If the king prove unworthy, the glory, wisdom and strength typified by the anointing on head, breast and arms will be taken from him. Foliot has another view. In his eyes the anointing sets the king apart from other men and gives him power to judge even ecclesiastics; he details five anointings, and specifies the use of chrism which makes the king another Christ—an interesting and no doubt tendencious reference, for chrism, the oil used for holy orders and consecrations, had been discontinued at the instance of the reforming papacy both in the Empire and in England, and the less sacred oil of catechumens had been substituted. Henry himself had been anointed with the inferior oil, but it is worth remarking that there is evidence that chrism was used at the coronation of the young Henry in 1170, when Foliot was present.

---

[1] For Gerhoh's doctrine (*M.G.H.*, Libelli de Lite, III) *v. De Novitatibus*, xii, pp. 264-7, 300-1; *De Investigatione Antichristi*, xxv, xxvii, pp. 833 *et seqq.*; cf. also *De Edificio Dei*, xiii, xiv, xvii, xxv, pp. 142-5, 148-50, 154. *V. supra* pp. 82-4.

(v)

Looking back for the last time upon the English bishops of 1160-70, the impression remains, even after all the shocks and frustrations of the great quarrel, that they were an unusually distinguished and honourable body of men. All the bishops of the province of Canterbury, with the possible exceptions of Nigel of Ely and Jocelin of Salisbury, were quite free during these years from the two cancers that so often ravaged the medieval clergy—impurity of life and luxurious wealth. Moreover all, with the same exception, were essentially men of the Church to whom ecclesiastical affairs and interests took precedence of all else. Even the three—Gilbert Foliot, Hilary and Jocelin— who identified themselves most closely with the king's party retained a freedom of outlook and action very different from that of regalist bishops in other ages and countries. They were never royal clerks in the sense that several members of the episcopate were in the later decades of the century. It is hard to avoid the conclusion that this state of things was very largely due to the freedom which the Church had enjoyed under Stephen and to the surveillance exercised by Theobald and Thomas in his first years. Above all, they were potentially a more closely knit and manageable body for the archbishop than any other between the days of Lanfranc and those of Stephen Langton. Steeped as they were in the ideas of the post-Gregorian reformers they would have been, in more peaceful days, the agents of a great renewal under an archbishop who might have applied, undistracted, to his ecclesiastical office the energy and talents which he had shown as chancellor.

Even in the evil days in which their lot was cast their *rôle* was important and even decisive. What Henry II would have achieved after 1162 with an archbishop as pliant as his chancellor had been and with a hierarchy recruited from men of the type of Geoffrey Ridel, John of Oxford and Richard of Ilchester must remain a matter for conjecture. Probably the forces making for uniformity and centralization in the Church—the papacy itself, the rationalized canon law, the schools and universities—would have proved too strong to resist, and would have soon overthrown the barriers of a regional or insular church of the early Norman model had it been re-established in England. Nevertheless a resolute attempt was made to set up such a system in England under Henry II. That it failed not only in the extreme and revolutionary form to which Henry had recourse in the anger of the quarrel, but also in the more moderate design of gathering into the king's hands the political and judicial control of the Church, was due in the first place to his failure to find an archbishop who would act as his deputy, but it was due also to the reluctance of the English bishops to abandon the close relationship with Rome and the duty of obedience to metropolitan and Pope, even against the command of the king, which they had learned in their younger days in the schools and had practised as officials and bishops under the guidance of archbishop Theobald.

APPENDIX I: BISHOPS OCCUPYING ENGLISH SEES 1163—1170

The dates, unless otherwise noted, are as in *Handbook of British Chronology*

SEE	NAME	DATES OF BIRTH (APPROXIMATE)	CONSECRATION	DEATH OR TRANSLATION
CANTERBURY	Thomas Becket	?1117/8	3 June, 1160	29 Dec., 1170
Bath (& Wells)	Robert	?	1136	31 Aug., 1166
Chichester	Hilary	?	3 Aug., 1147	19 July, 1169
Ely	Nigel	? circa 1095	1 Oct., 1133	30 May, 1169
Exeter	Bartholomew	? circa 1110	summer, 1161[1]	15 Dec., 1184
Hereford	Gilbert Foliot	? circa 1110	5 Sept., 1148	transl. 1163
	Robert of Melun	circa 1100	12 Dec., 1163	27 Feb., 1167
Lichfield (Chester & Coventry)	Richard Peche	?	between autumn 1160 and 18 April, 1161[2]	6 Oct., 1182
Lincoln	Robert de Chesney	circa 1095	19 Dec., 1148	27 Dec., 1166
London	Gilbert Foliot		1163	18 Feb., 1187
Norwich	William de Turbe	circa 1095	1147[3]	17 Jan., 1174
Rochester	Walter	circa 1105-10	14 Mar., 1148	26 July, 1182
Salisbury	Jocelin de Bohun	circa 1105	1142[4]	18 Nov., 1184
Winchester	Henry of Blois	circa 1095	17 Nov., 1129	9 Aug., 1171
Worcester	Roger	circa 1133	23 Aug., 1164	9 Aug., 1174
YORK	Roger of Pont l'Evêque	circa 1115	10 Oct., 1154	26 Nov., 1181
Carlisle	(vacant)			
Durham	Hugh du Puiset	circa 1125	20 Dec., 1153	3 Mar., 1195

1 So with great probability Morey, *Bartholomew of Exeter*, 13.

2 John of Salisbury, *ep.* 78, implies the vacancy of Lichfield; the other is the limiting date of the *Handbook*.

3 The date usually given is 1146; 1147 is given by *Chron. Min.* of St Benet's of Hulme, in John Oxenede (Rolls Series), *sub anno*.

4 The only evidence for the year is *Annal. Margan. sub. anno. Handbook* has 1141-2.

THE GENEALOGY OF JOCELIN DE BOHUN OF SALISBURY

OPPOSITE is the skeleton of the Bohun family tree as it applies to Jocelin and his relation Savaric, bishop of Bath. It follows the tree found among the papers of the late L. C. Loyd, and kindly lent to me by Professor D. C. Douglas.

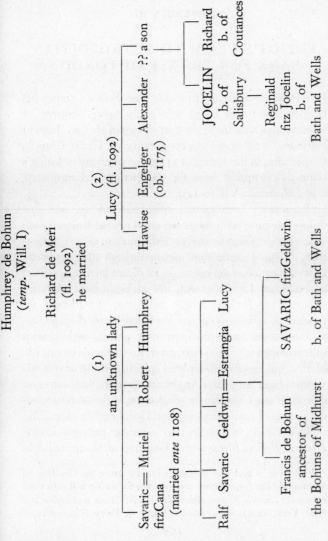

Humphrey de Bohun
(*temp.* Will. I)

Richard de Meri
(fl. 1092)
he married

(1)
an unknown lady

Savaric = Muriel   Robert   Humphrey
fitzCana
(married *ante* 1108)

Ralf   Savaric   Geldwin = Estrangia   Lucy

Francis de Bohun   SAVARIC fitzGeldwin
ancestor of   b. of Bath and Wells
the Bohuns of Midhurst

(2)
Lucy (fl. 1092)

Hawise   Engelger   Alexander   ?? a son
(ob. 1175)

JOCELIN   Richard
b. of   b. of
Salisbury   Coutances

Reginald
fitz Jocelin
b. of
Bath and Wells

Note: The two literary data concerning the relationship of Jocelin to other members of his family (apart from his brother and son) are William FitzStephen's statement that Engelger de Bohun was his *patruus* (*Materials,* III 129), and that his son Reginald was Savaric's near relation (*avunculus vester*) in *Epistolae Cantuarienses,* (Rolls Series), cccxiv, p. 361. Loyd, as stated in the text, set Jocelin in the position indicated above, and then cancelled the entry without substituting another.

FOLIOT'S CLAIM TO METROPOLITAN RANK FOR THE SEE OF LONDON

IT would seem highly probable that Foliot's somewhat hesitant claim was based principally upon Geoffrey of Monmouth's account of the past glories of the see. John of Salisbury, writing to the community of Christ Church, Canterbury, in the spring of 1169, and referring to Foliot's claim to exemption from the jurisdiction of Canterbury, says (*Materials*, VII 10-11):

'Ecce enim Londiniensis episcopus publice, non sine dolore fidelium, protestatus est, quod primae Britanniarum sedi, videlicet Cantuariensi ecclesiae, nullam debet obedientiam, et quod cathedram metropoliticam illuc transferri faciet ubi eam esse debere fingit, ne dicam mentitur, scilicet ad ecclesiam Londiniensem, ubi archiflaminem gloriatur sedisse dum Jovialis religio colebatur. Et fortasse vir prudens et religiosus cultum Jovis instaurare disponit, ut, si alio modo archiepiscopari non potest, archiflaminis saltem nomen et titulum assequatur. Fretus tamen est oraculo Merlini, qui, nescio quo repletus spiritu, perhibetur ante adventum beati Augustini Anglorum apostoli, vaticinatus est delendam esse Christianam religionem, et denuo reformandam quando Londiniensis dignitas Doroberniam adornabit.'

This clearly refers to two separate passages in the *Historia Regum Britanniae* of Geoffrey of Monmouth.[1] In

---

[1] There is a vast and ever-growing literature on Geoffrey of Monmouth, but for ordinary purposes the following will suffice for reference: *Historia Regum Britanniae*, ed. A. Griscom (London and New York, 1929); *Vita Merlini*, ed. J. J. Parry (University of

the first of these (Faral, pp. 144-5; Griscom, pp. 329-30)
the story is told of the evangelization of Britain by Faganus
and Duuianus under Pope Eleutherius and King Lucius:

'Fuerunt tunc in brittania xxviii flamines set et ii archiflamines . . . hos etiam ex precepto apostolici ydolatriam
(*sic;* a variant reading gives *ydolatriae*) eripuerunt, et ubi
erant flamines episcopos ubi archiflamines archiepiscopos
posuerunt. Sedes autem archiflaminum in tribus nobilibus
ciuitatibus fuerunt . . . Lundoniis videlicet atque eboraci et
in urbe legionum . . . Lundoniensi metropolitano submissa
est loegria et cornubia.'

The second passage occurs in the Prophecy of Merlin,
originally a separate composition of Geoffrey, which was
later incorporated into the *Historia Regum* (Faral, p. 191;
Griscom, p. 385):

'Mox ille (*sc.* Merlinus) in fletum erumpens spiritum
hausit prophetie et ait . . . delebitur iterum religio et trans-
mutatio primarum sedium fiet. Dignitas lundonie adornabit
doroberniam et pastor eboracensis septimus in armorico
regno frequentabitur. Menevia pallio urbis legionum
induetur.'

There can be no doubt that John of Salisbury is quoting
Geoffrey, and the verbal reminiscences of the two passages
are so close that he must either have had the text of the
Historia, or some writing or utterance of Foliot, before him
as he wrote. He favoured other correspondents with a
similar account, for we find the bishop of Paris, Maurice,
passing the information on to Alexander III (*Materials*,
VII 41). Mlle Foreville (*L'Egliseetla Royautéen Angleterre*,

Illinois Studies in Language and Literature, X 3, 1925); E. Faral,
La Légende Arthurienne, in Bibliothéque de l'Ecole des Hautes
Etudes, 3 vols., Paris, 1929. Griscom and Faral (in his vol. 3) have
texts of the *Historia*.

288 and notes) regards the whole passage as a jest of John's, one more example of that English humour which she found typified in the letter *Multiplicem*, but it is difficult to believe that John of Salisbury would broadcast a *jeu d'esprit* over two countries at such a crisis of the archbishop's fortunes, and so disguised that the bishop of Paris would retail it in all seriousness to Alexander III. When it is remembered that Robert de Chesney, Foliot's uncle, was Geoffrey's patron, and that he had dedicated to the bishop shortly after 1148 his *Vita Merlini*,[1] it is difficult to avoid the conclusion, not only that Foliot must have known the works of Geoffrey well, but that he must also have regarded them (as have indeed several modern scholars) as embodying valuable traditions, otherwise unknown, of the condition of things in England before the days of Augustine of Canterbury.

---

[1] For the dedication of the *Vita Merlini* to Robert of Lincoln, *v.* Faral, vol. 2, pp. 29 *et seqq.* The accepted date for the first redaction of the *Historia*, accepted by both Faral and Griscom, is April, 1136; that of the *Vita Merlini* is 1148 or shortly after.

THE CHRONOLOGY OF THE COUNCIL OF NORTHAMPTON

THERE is some confusion among the chroniclers as to the date of the council of Northampton, but there would appear to be a very fair probability that the correct date and sequence of events are given by William FitzStephen, who was himself present and who accounts for each day and its business. It may be added that his indications of the days of the week are correct for the year 1164. His detailed notices are on pp. 50-6 of his *Life*. FitzStephen did not follow the archbishop into exile, and he was soon reconciled with the king. He had therefore the opportunity (if he used it) to make, preserve and discuss any notes or recollections without the disturbing and sudden moves that would have affected the archbishop's closer companions, such as Herbert of Bosham.

According to FitzStephen the council was summoned for the octave of St Michael, being a Tuesday (i.e., 6th October), and on that day the archbishop arrived at Northampton. The following day he waited on the king after Mass, but no general meeting took place; the first business was on Thursday, 8th October. Thenceforward FitzStephen gives continuous indications (*die tertia, quarta, quinta, sexta*, &c.) and specifies that it was on a Monday that Thomas was incapacitated by illness. After narrating the archbishop's flight, he notes (p. 70) that he remained in England from the fifteenth day after St Michael (i.e., 13th October) to the second day of November, and that on that day, All Soul's Day, he crossed to France.

This reckoning, which is certainly clear and consistent, is not followed by the other biographers and chroniclers, who are curiously vague and uninformative, save for Herbert of Bosham, who, as will be seen, presents difficulties of another kind. Thus Ralph of Diceto, a very careful writer who was present at Northampton, notes only (I 313) that the archbishop 'praesentiam suam exhibuit apud Northantunam iii idus Octobris' (i.e., October 13th). Diceto, however, gives a very short account of the council, and his accuracy may perhaps be vindicated on the supposition that he wished to avoid all complexity and therefore selected for notice only the decisive, critical day.

Gervase of Canterbury, on the other hand, who was not present, and was, indeed, only a child at the time, is probably in real error. He states that the council opened 'die tertia ante festum S. Kalixti' (I 186), which would be Monday, 12th October, the day that the archbishop spent ill in bed, and then continues to give a fairly full day-to-day account which would take the break-up of the council several days beyond Tuesday, 13th October.

A more serious problem is provided by Herbert of Bosham. He was of course present, but he departed on an embassy for the archbishop immediately, and wrote his *Life* some twenty years after the event. He bases his chronology on the assumption that the feast of St Calixtus (14th October) fell on the critical Tuesday of the council. Tuesday, however, in 1164 was 13th October, and it seems impossible to account for Bosham's reckoning save as a sheer mistake. His mind was obviously not perfectly clear, for he begins with a hesitant remark (*Materials*, III 296): 'Tempus, ni fallor, mensis Octobris hebdomadae feria quinta, sexta ante beati Calixti papae et martyris natalitium diem'. The opening phrase is not easy to construe, and it is

possible that here, as in subsequent passages, a scribe has
tampered with Bosham's text in order to eliminate a difficult
date. Bosham then continues with a day-to-day narrative in
which he agrees with FitzStephen in the main outline from
Thursday to Tuesday. When he comes (p. 301) to Tuesday,
'tertia videlicet feria, quae vulgo die Martis dicitur', one
MS adds the interlinear note (which may have been in
Bosham's text) 'die beati Calixti papae martyris'. The
assumption that Tuesday was the feast of St Calixtus gives
further trouble when he has to explain how the archbishop
could say a votive Mass of St Stephen on a double feast. He
says (p. 304): 'Et hanc quidem missam, die qui festus non
erat, cum pallio celebravit, nisi quia beati Calixti papae et
martyris natalitium fuit'. Once again the sense is not clear,
and one MS reads for 'die qui' the words 'eo die quia', and
it is possible that the text as printed in *Materials* is faulty.
Bosham then continues, after describing the incidents of
the archbishop's wanderings (pp. 324-5): 'Die vero
Animarum, qui fuit tertia feria, quintus decimus dies ab illa
tertia feria, ab illo die Martis, quo apud Northantune pug-
narat ad bestias . . . intravit mare'. This, as the editor points
out, involves a double error. All Souls in 1164 fell on a
Monday, and it was one day less than three weeks from the
decisive day of the council (13th October). Moreover,
Bosham's own account of the archbishop's journey to the
coast, which he narrates in greater detail than any other
source, cannot be reconciled with his allowance of a bare
fortnight. Thus he says of the stay at Sempringham
(actually at Hoyland, a hermitage of Sempringham) 'tres
dies securius latitabat (p. 324)', and of the journey from
Haverholme to Eastry (*ibid.*): 'nocte ibat et die latitabat,
octo noctibus dierum conficiens iter', while at Eastry (*ibid.*):
'latuit . . . usque ad diem animarum diebus octo'. Even

when allowance is made for some ambiguity (e.g., as to whether the eight days at Eastry include the days of arrival and departure), we already have more than a fortnight accounted for, and there are still several (? 3-4) days needed for the journey from Northampton to Lincoln, and then to Hoyland by water. In other words, Bosham's account, the details of which tally with scattered indications in other *Lives*, is inconsistent with his own dating, though not with that of FitzStephen. The conclusion would seem to be that in default of further evidence, the account of FitzStephen must be accepted as in the main correct.

THE ARCHBISHOP'S ILLNESS
on the night of Sunday-Monday, October 11th-12th, 1164.

THE historian's interest is naturally aroused by this illness, which came so suddenly and unexpectedly, and departed as rapidly, the more so as the partizans of Henry suggested at the time that it was feigned. This charge may be dismissed at once, but it is natural to ask whether it was physiological and organic, or whether it was psychogenetic, the result of the as yet unresolved conflict and apprehension under which the archbishop laboured. The answer, could it be given, would be of value for any estimate of Archbishop Thomas's character.

The following is the evidence of the *Lives*. The order followed is the probable chronological order of composition, but it must be remembered that FitzStephen and Bosham were the only biographers certainly present at Northampton, though others drew upon first-hand witnesses.

William of Canterbury (*Materials*, I 32):

'Iliaca passione, qua saepius laborabat, vexari coepit, adeo ut lecto affigeretur ... Et quia putabatur aegritudo fingi,' &c.

Grim (II 392):

(On the Sunday evening)

'Gravi mox tactus dolore splenis, lecto decubuit, noctemque sine cibo et insomnem ducens, miserabili decoctus dolore, vix diem praestolatus est. Solebat hoc modo vexari, sed nunc anxius solito, turbato nimirum sanguine post iras diurnas et litigia ... Suspicatus denique rex ne forte affectata esset infirmitas,' &c.

I Anonymous (IV 44):

'Et ecce citra noctis medium, cum vir Domini post anxietatem et laborem quieti se dedisset, vehemens dolor lateris eum arripuit, et tota nocte illa cum diei sequentis parte non modica graviter afflixit. Frequenter namque ita pati consueverat, sed et tunc propter anxietatem, quam die praeterita pertulerat, dolor ejus renovatus est.'

Guernes (ed. Walberg, lines 1508-11; 1513):

'Quant ço vint vers lu seir, a l'ostel s'en ala.
Li mals del flanc le prist, jur et nuit li dura.
Achaisunus en eut, e suvent lui greva,
Par cel' ire qu'il out, dunc lui renovela . . .
Il dit n'i puest aler, d'anguisse tressura.'

Will. FitzStephen (III 56):

'Sexta die, languor repente (ut fit) ortus eum moratus est, quo minus ad curiam iret. Siquidem renes ejus frigore et dolore contremuerunt; oportuitque cervicalia calefacere, et vicissim opponere.'

Herbert of Bosham (III 300-1):

'Verum archipraesul ea die, in ipsa etiam nocte diei, gravissime illa quae iliaca dicitur percussus est passione. Sed rex et qui in aula fictum hoc, non veram infirmitatem arbitrantes,' &c.

I submitted this evidence to two medical friends. Their answers, given independently, were identical, viz., that in their opinion the symptoms were consistent with, and perhaps indicative of, renal colic due to the presence of renal calculus. While one was of opinion that severe mental strain might cause the attack, the other considered that some physical shock was needed, but this might have occurred either through some simple strain on horseback, or by a digestive ailment brought on by exhaustion or strain.

THE PLAN OF NORTHAMPTON CASTLE

THE medieval castle of Northampton stood immediately to the east of the present main (the sometime L. & N.W.R.) railway station, which is indeed known as the 'Castle station'. Considerable ruins remained, though gradually decreasing, in the eighteenth and nineteenth centuries, but these were finally swept away in 1880, when the station was enlarged and a goods yard was added to the east of the line. Fortunately, plans and photographs are in existence, though the site was never scientifically excavated, and it is possible to reconstruct the original plan with some certainty (*V. C. H. Northampton*, III 34 *et seq*).

The castle at the time of the council seems to have been of the normal motte-and-bailey type, with a mound and tower at the north, near which was the main gate into the castle-yard, which was surrounded by a curtain wall. To the south-west of the enclosure, and abutting on to the wall, was the residential building. This, in castles of this type and date, was a hall (*aula*) sometimes of a single storey, sometimes of two storeys, in both cases usually above cellarage. There is no certain evidence that there was a keep at Northampton. The accounts, and in particular that of Herbert of Bosham, make it clear that there were two storeys, the lower, on or near ground-level, containing the hall proper (*aula*) and an inner room (*camera*), the upper consisting of at least one large room, reached by stairs probably ascending either externally or from the inner room. There was also a chapel, probably, as often in such castles, set at an angle to the main building, between it and the outer wall. The following indications are given by the biographers.

On Wednesday, 7th October, Thomas went to the castle to see the king; the latter was hearing Mass; the archbishop was accordingly shown into an outer room, which may have communicated with the chapel (Fitz-Stephen, III 50: 'In cameram primam intromissus, sedit regem exspectans'). On the following Tuesday, he rode through the outer gate, and dismounted at the entrance to the hall (FitzStephen, III 57: 'Intraturus in aulam castri, cum equo descendisset'). It was here that Foliot and others awaited him (FitzStephen, 57: 'aderat ibi ad ostium aulae'; Bosham, III 305: 'ut aulam ingreditur'). The king had previously retreated to an inner room, which we learn was upstairs (Bosham, 305: 'Rex autem, qui in coenaculo seorsum', &c. *Ibid.*, 307: 'cum aliqui de coenaculo, in quo rex cum suis erat, ad inferiorem domum in qua nos eramus descendisset', &c. cf. *ibid.* and 309 for communication between those upstairs and those below). The I Anonymous corroborates (IV 46): having passed through the gate 'porta', Thomas alighted at the door ('ad januas desiliens') and passed through the hall to an inner room ('aulam ingressus pertransiit, et in ulteriorem domum pervenit. Porro rex cum familiaribus suis in remotiori camera consistebat'). He adds that the faggots over which Thomas tripped were in the hall, no doubt by the central hearth. As regards size, the inner room was large enough to hold the archbishop, his two clerks and the other bishops; the upper room held the king and all his councillors. As foundations and fragments found at Northampton prove, the domestic building there was of stone; it was probably strongly and even elaborately constructed, in the manner common at the time, and surviving in numerous examples (cf. A. Hamilton Thompson, *English Military Architecture* [Oxford, 1912]).

THE LETTER *MULTIPLICEM*

THE celebrated letter *Multiplicem nobis* (*ep.* ccxxv in *Materials*, ed J. C. Robertson, V 521-44), ostensibly written by Gilbert Foliot to the archbishop in the late summer of 1166, shortly after reading *epp.* ccxxiii-iv from Archbishop Thomas to the clergy of England and himself, has been challenged as spurious by a number of historians during the past century-and-a-half. Branded as a forgery, or at least as highly suspicious, by Lingard and other Catholic or Anglo-Catholic writers, who felt it was damaging to the reputation of the archbishop and saint, it was accepted as genuine by J. C. Robertson in his early Life of Becket,[1] and printed as such by him among the letters a quarter of a century later. Robertson, however, unwittingly confused subsequent historians by the inadequate account he gave of his manuscript materials,[2] and the French biographer, Dom A. L'Huillier, devoted considerable space to what he considered a convincing demonstration of the forgery, while the latest historian of the controversy, Mlle R. Foreville, whose large volume appeared in 1943, treats the letter with the utmost disdain; it appears in her index

---

[1] J. C. Robertson, in *Becket, Archbishop of Canterbury* (London, 1859), Appendix vi, p. 325, gives, with references, the opinions of historians to the date of writing. Of those who impugn the authenticity he remarks 'their arguments are very weak', but he nowhere enters upon a full discussion.

[2] *Materials*, V introd., xxii-xxiv, and p. 521 note *a*. His description of the Cave MS is certainly misleading; he seems not to have realized either its early date or its intrinsic interest or its significance for the letter *Multiplicem*.

as 'pseudo-Foliot' and she refers to it throughout as a palpable fraud, a literary squib which was not meant to be taken seriously by anyone—in fact, an early specimen of typical British humour.[1] As the letter is of considerable interest in the history of the controversy and is, if genuine, by far the most important piece of evidence we possess for judging Foliot and his case (and by implication, that of the archbishop), the question seems to merit full consideration.

Before beginning, however, it may be well to make it clear why this letter—alone of the whole corpus—should have been attacked by the critics. Two reasons, the one of circumstance, the other of sentiment, have contributed to bring this about. The letter was not contained in the first edition of the letters by Lupus (the Augustinian Fr Christian Wolf) which appeared at Brussels in 1682, for no other reason than its absence from the Vatican manuscript (1220) from which he printed. It was first published, from an English manuscript, by Lord Lyttelton as an Appendix to his *Life of Henry II* (1773-7 [Vol II, pp.67-71, 185-99 Appendix and Notes]). It thus appeared to be without credentials and, in fact, has never been critically examined with full reference to the manuscripts. Consequently, it was treated by writers of the nineteenth century as a document that could be attacked or defended on its contents alone, and as from the first it was regarded (somewhat strangely) as a piece of evidence highly damaging to Archbishop Thomas, it was impugned by Lingard, R. H. Froude and other writers of Catholic sympathies and as eagerly accepted by Lord Campbell and others of the Protestant school. It thus became a party rallying point,

[1] Dom A. L'Huillier, *Saint Thomas de Cantorbéry*, 2 vols., Paris, 1891-2. Cf. vol. i Note B, pp. 425-32. Raymonde Foreville, *L'Eglise et La Royauté en Angleterre sous Henri II Plantagenet* (Paris, 1943), 244-7.

and it was strongly attacked in an openly partizan spirit by Dom L'Huillier. Mlle Foreville's partizanship is not so obvious, and it would appear that she was convinced in essentials by her compatriot's arguments. The two French scholars are indeed most emphatic. Dom L'Huillier gives as his judgment: 'Il est trop clair que le pamphlet n'est qu'un factum méprisable et sans authorité' (p.428), and asking himself the question, 'Gilbert Foliot est-il vraiment l'auteur de ce libelle?', he answers: 'Il nous est impossible de la croire' (429). The letter is, in fact, 'Une amplification maladroite de la lettre des évêques' (430). And he concludes: 'Nous avons démontré surtout que c'était un document sans aucune valeur historique'. Mlle Foreville, after expressing general sympathy with Dom L'Huillier, gives her judgment (p. 247): 'Nous avons affaire à un vaste pamphlet humoristique ... c'est en somme un divertissement littéraire qui, dès le xiie siècle, nous donne une parfaite image de l'humour britannique'.

I. *The evidence of the manuscripts.* This, though it is the crucial witness, has strangely enough never been set out. Robertson, though a conscientious editor whose critical judgment was in the main sound, is inadequate, and indeed positively misleading, in his account of the MSS he used. Dom L'Huillier, a monk of Solesmes, never examined the manuscripts and frankly admitted this; Mlle Foreville has done no more than read Robertson, whom she has misunderstood.[1]

[1] She remarks (p. 247, note 2): 'Le pamphlet (i.e. *Multiplicem*) ... ne se trouve pas dans le plus ancien recueil des lettres, celui d'Alain de Tewkesbury ... Dans d'autres, le texte en est donné à la fin et d'une autre écriture'. MS Vatican 1220 is only one (and that neither the archetype nor the most reliable) of the MSS of Alan's collection. MS Bodley 249 (Cave) has the letter at the end, but this need not arouse suspicion, as a number of hands have already con-

In the first place, it must be recognized that there was no medieval canon of the Becket correspondence. The great collection of Alan of Tewkesbury did indeed exist from the beginning, but it was not complete and was manifestly faulty in its arrangement. Alongside of it existed other dossiers, such as that of Foliot and of the Curia, together with collections of letters and miscellaneous items, and others very early made collections as supplements to or substitutes for that of Alan. Nor have we the actual manuscript compiled or passed by Alan; all manuscripts of the collection differ more or less from one another. Consequently, the only and sufficient guarantee of the authenticity of individual pieces is good manuscript authority; absence from one or more of the existing collections is no proof of forgery.

The letter *Multiplicem nobis* is found in at least three manuscripts of the twelfth and thirteenth centuries: Bodley MS Cave, e Musaeo 249; Bodley MS Douce, 287; and Brit. Mus. MS Cotton, Claudius B II.

(*a*) The Cave MS 249 is a collection of letters and documents for the most part written by, or addressed to, Gilbert Foliot. It is written in a number of different hands, all contemporary with one another and dating from the last quarter of the xii century. It gives every sign of London provenance and, indeed, those best fitted to judge have thought that it was compiled by members of Foliot's *familia*, either after his death or even during the last years of his life.[1]

---

tributed to the book. In MS Bodley Douce 287 the letter is in a normal place among the letters and in the hand of the copyist of its neighbours.

[1] Dr R. W. Hunt, Keeper of the Western MSS at the Bodleian Library, was kind enough to inspect the MS after I had done so, and

The letter *Multiplicem* does not occur in its logical or chronological place in the series; it is written in a hand found nowhere else in the book and it begins on the last page of a quire. It is, therefore, physically an addition to the collection. But the hand is a contemporary one; it is not an addition made years later by a reader from another source. Whatever may be the explanation of its position, the occurrence of the letter in a collection made in the interests of Foliot, and by those with access to his papers and within a few years (at most) of his death, is very strong evidence of authenticity.

(*b*) MS Douce 287. This is a late xii century collection of material connected with St Thomas, probably made either at or on behalf of, or at any rate soon to be given to, Lesnes Abbey, founded in 1178 in honour of the saint by Richard de Lucy.

(*c*) Cotton Claudius B II. This is a Canterbury manuscript of the early xiiith century, made up of material connected with Archbishop Thomas, chiefly a version of Alan's collection. Robertson (V xii) used it as the basis of his edition, judging it 'of far greater value' than the Vatican MS used by Lupus.[1] The letter *Multiplicem* appears in its natural place, immediately after the letter of the archbishop to Foliot, as printed by Robertson.

---

to write: 'The writing (of *Multiplicem*) is certainly contemporary with the rest of the volume, and without ever having analysed the volume in detail, it has all the appearance of a collection of letters made by someone in close touch with Foliot. I am tempted to say by a member of his *familia*. I should not say, therefore, that its position in the volume was enough to condemn it'. This view is shared by Mr C. N. L. Brooke.

[1] Robertson, V introd. xxii.

In addition, as remarked by Robertson, *Multiplicem* occurs twice in the index of Vatican MS 1220, thus indicating its presence in the manuscript used by the copyist; it does not occur, however, either in the index or the body of Corpus Christi College, Cambridge, MS295, a manuscript hitherto not used by any editor of the correspondence. This is a Canterbury book of the early xiiith century, not unlike Claudius B II.

II. *The internal evidence.*

(*a*) The letter purports to be written by one intimately connected with the whole sequence of events of 1161-4 in England; he gives details known from no other source (e.g., the inclusion of the bishops at Clarendon in a single room; the violence of the king's supporters; the archbishop's sudden change without consulting his colleagues) or such that no one save a very close participant could have known (e.g., the king's command at Northampton, after Thomas's departure, but when, as we know, Foliot was present as his counsellor, not to molest the fugitive). There are indeed throughout numerous touches which could only be given by a *bona fide* witness.

(*b*) The writer of *Multiplicem* had before him and vividly in his consciousness the two letters of the primate, *Fraternitatis vestrae* to the bishops and *Mirandum* to Foliot (*epp.* ccxxiii, ccxxiv), immediately preceding *Multiplicem* in Robertson's edition. Cf. *ep.* ccxxiii, p. 493: 'Accingimi... adversus eos qui quaerunt tollere animam ecclesiae, quae est libertas', and Foliot, p. 525: 'Sic ... libertatem ecclesiae ... ademisitis; quae si vita ejus est, ut scribitis', &c.

Ibid., 491: 'Unum vobis dico... ut resumeretis vires, qui conversi estis retrorsum in die belli, si forte saltem aliquis ex omnibus vobis ascenderet ex adverso, opponeret se murum pro domo Israel', and Foliot, 528: 'Vestra nobis exprobratur epistola quod in die belli conversi sumus, quod ex adverso non ascendimus, quod nos murum pro domo Domini non opposuimus', &c.

Ep. ccxxiv, p. 512: 'Non sani igitur capitis esse dignoscitur qui intentat ei [*sc.* ecclesiae] ruinam, homini similis montem magnum fune circumligatum tentanti deicere', and Foliot, 523: 'Cernentes ecclesiae jus subverti, fas nefasque confundi, montis illius magni quem dicitis deorsum cacumen inflecti', &c.

(c) Twice in Foliot's letter there are hidden quotations from the Rule of St Benedict: (i) p. 526: 'Virtus est peccato, cum exsurgit, occurrere, mentisque sinistros foetus ad petram, quae Christus est, statim cum nascuntur, allidere'. Cf. *Regula S Benedicti*, Prologue. (ii) p. 540: 'Haec itaque non fervore novitio sed maturo fuerant attendenda consilio'. Cf. *Regula*, cap. I: 'non fervore novitio'. Foliot as monk and abbot would know the Rule almost by heart, and these concealed references are wholly in his style; cf. similar concealed references to the Second Book of St Gregory's Dialogues (Life of St Benedict) in *epp.* xi and cix (*v. supra* p. 42, n. 1).

III. The arguments against authenticity of Dom L'Huillier and Mlle Foreville are drawn from statements in *Multiplicem* which are, so it is said, so contrary to historical truth as to be inconceivable as coming from the pen of Foliot. In Dom L'Huillier's words (p. 427): 'L'interminable lettre...n'est qu'un tissu de contradictions et de démentis donnés aux faits les mieux établis'. That the letter contains tendencious and mutually inconsistent statements need not be denied, but they are not the blunders of ignorance but the perversions of an angry partizan. Controversialists, especially when the struggle is one of vital issues between embittered parties, rarely confine themselves to a sober statement of fact; even in England within the last hundred years it would be possible to compile a collection of very violent and questionable statements from ecclesiastics as well as from politicians who have stood high in the estimation of their countrymen. Actually, however, the *démentis* of Dom L'Huillier are not so numerous or so serious as he suggests: (i) The accusation that Thomas bought the chancellorship (V 523-4), scouted by Dom L'Huillier, is, as Mlle Foreville admits (p. 247), very plausible; (ii) The alleged speedy return from France in 1161 (V 524), which is said to be contrary to the sources, can be reconciled with them and would seem to be borne out by entries in the Pipe Roll of 1160-1 (Henry II), pp. 56, 57, 58, etc.; (iii) The statement in the letter, p. 524, that Foliot, when he opposed the election of Thomas to Canterbury, 'verbum illico proscriptionis audivimus, et exsilio crudeliter addicti sumus; nec solum persona nostra, sed et domus patris mei, et conjuncta nobis affinitas et cognatio tota', has been understood, by Dom L'Huillier and Mlle Foreville, to imply that the bishop and his relatives were actually exiled—which they certainly were not—and hence to be a forger's or parodist's clumsy reminiscence of what actually happened to Thomas. But the Latin need mean no more than that Henry made the threat, to take effect if Foliot persisted in opposition, and it is not impossible that he should have threatened against Foliot the move which he later carried into execution with his rival; (iv) Finally, it is argued that the encomiums on Henry and his family in the letter are so fantastic as to be inconceivable if intended to be taken seriously. Whether in fact they are notably more fantastic than those in the letter *Quae vestro, pater*

(V 408-13) of the bishops to Thomas, in which John of Salisbury recognized at once Foliot's hand, is a matter of opinion; but we know that the bishop of London's authentic statements regarding Henry appeared to John so extravagant as to provoke his *Quaere peregrinum!*

IV. Whether *Multiplicem* is written in a style which is, or is not, similar to that of Foliot's other letters must be a matter of opinion. It would be very difficult to subject the diffuse and somewhat toneless, but correct and arid, Latinity of Foliot to the tests of *clausulae* and vocabulary which are possible with a highly individual stylist such as Tacitus or Tertullian. Dom L'Huillier (p. 430) writes that 'la différence est frappante'. To the present writer, after many years' familiarity with Foliot and his celebrated letter, the similarity appears exact. A more competent witness, Mr C. N. L. Brooke, who has for several years been engaged upon an edition of Foliot's letters, is of the same opinion. 'The forceful style', he writes, 'the restraint which builds up to a flurry of complicated rhetorical questions; the argument, at times as terse and effective as one of Lanfranc's, but for ever going off down byways and ending in a quagmire of irrelevant quotations . . . it is all very characteristic of Gilbert'.

V. If the letter was not written by Foliot, who was the author and why did he write? Dom L'Huillier thinks it was written by a regalist clerk to discredit the archbishop; Mlle Foreville, as has been seen, regards the whole thing as a *jeu d'esprit*—or something more ponderous—and suggests John of Salisbury as the writer. Even granted that any example of subtle and ironic parody on such a scale could be quoted in the whole of medieval Latin literature, it is impossible to suggest a motive that could have inspired John, or any other of the archbishop's exiled and devoted clerks, to compose an imaginary letter which cut so cruelly at their master.

The letter *Multiplicem* is assuredly a strange document— perhaps the strangest, as it is certainly among the most brilliant, of the whole corpus of the controversy. It is indeed an enigma, a two-edged sword that cuts the archbishop so sharply that his advocates for more than a century have endeavoured to discredit it, yet one also which, when regarded closely, pierces him who wields it with an envenomed point more fell than all the cuts of the archbishop's lash and the rapier thrusts of John of Salisbury. For it is Foliot whom *Multiplicem* damages incomparably more than Thomas: the faults of the latter which it catalogues had been already confessed and shriven; the faults of the writer which it reveals were hidden from his sight by a veil of his own weaving. As a literary composition it must remain, with all its blemishes, a rhetorical masterpiece, but its cold and unrelenting hatred, which cannot pardon error or understand generosity, comes from the abundance of a heart in which humility and love had long ceased to harbour.

INDEX

Date Due

FE 1 1 '66		
NO 20 68		
NO 23 '70		
JY 28 '71		
OCT 27 '78		
MAY 17 74		
	PRINTED IN U. S. A.	